MW01630309

FERRARI
275GTB & GTS
2-cam, 4-cam; 'Competizione'; Spider

Osprey AutoHistory

FERRARI 275GTB & GTS

2-cam, 4-cam; 'Competizione'; Spider

IAN WEBB

Published in 1981 by Osprey Publishing Limited,
12–14 Long Acre, London WC2 9LP
Member company of the George Philip Group

United States distribution by

Osceola, Wisconsin 54020, USA

British Library Cataloguing in Publication Data

Webb, Ian
    Ferrari 275GTB & GTS.—(Autohistory)
    1. Ferrari automobile—History
    I. Title
    629.2′222   TL215.F47

ISBN 0-85045-402-6

Editor Tim Parker
Associate Michael Sedgwick
Photography Mirco Decet
Design Fred Price

Filmset and printed in England by
BAS Printers Limited, Over Wallop, Hampshire

Contents

Chapter 1
The final flowering

The final flowering of any design is generally the finest, and this was never more so than in the case of Ferrari's 275 range. Introduced in 1964, they were the ultimate development of the design philosophy that carried the Ferrari from relative obscurity in the immediate postwar days to the pinnacle of success on the race track and in the market place. By the time the 275 came along to set the seal on Commendatore Enzo Ferrari's early successes, a Ferrari car was not only the machine most likely to win any race of the era, it had also become the most desirable of luxury, not to say hedonistic, consumer durables—the equivalent in the sports car field of the Rolls-Royce among saloons.

Right *The discreet badge of the master-stylist*

Below *The traditional Ferrari script, with a stylized prancing horse added above it by a proud owner*

If, as this book continues, you form the impression that the author is a rabid enthusiast for the 275 you will not be wrong. I make no apology for lauding Ferraris in general and the 275 in particular. I will not apologise either for claiming to know their many shortcomings too, and being quite willing for these to appear in print. The most exciting cars, like the most interesting people, tend to have all kinds of more or less entertaining vices. A little, occasional character assassination as we discuss them will only add spice to the conversation.

Michael Parkes, whose development skills as an engineer at Ferrari did so much for the 275, starting from pole position in the 1961 Tourist Trophy at Goodwood. This was in Parkes' pre-Modena days, when he still worked in Britain. The car is a 250GT short wheelbase berlinetta, entered by UK importers Maranello Concessionaires. Behind is the similar Rob Walker-owned car of Stirling Moss

Overall, though, the 275 is a car deserving infinitely more praise than criticism. It is for my money the most satisfying driving machine ever made. It's not the fastest bar none, or possessed of the best roadholding of any car or even simply the best handling. And it is not the best looking. But in all the departments that count—road behaviour, longevity, looks, pure automotive aesthetics, and almost anything you care to name—it scores very high points. The result is a machine that, in total, is the finest combination of all these qualities. It wins on aggregate.

Neither is the 275 a car of compromise. As *Motor* magazine succinctly summed it up a few

years ago, when comparing a 275 with the Daytona that succeeded it, the 275 is probably the last car to come from the Ferrari factory in the days when Ferrari and his engineers made the kind of vehicle they thought you *needed*. Very, very adequate performance, brilliant handling and classic if old-fashioned lines took precedence, in their eyes, over such inconsequential matters as cockpit comfort. The brutal Daytona, by contrast, *Motor* labelled as the kind of Ferrari the factory thought you *wanted*.

What you need and what you want are not necessarily the same thing and the Daytona was totally different from—and in many ways nothing

The 250GTO, the first coupé to have a spoiler across the rear deck to help pin down the tail at speed, provided the inspiration for Pininfarina's rear-end treatment of the 275. The shape was repeated on the later 1964 GTO, then on the 275s

like so enjoyable as—the 275. Yes, air conditioning was available. And, yes, it was quiet (albeit not all *that* much quieter) in the cockpit. And definitely yes, the performance had gone from being marvellous to being monstrous—thus firmly putting those upstarts down the road at Automobili Ferruccio Lamborghini SpA in their parvenu place once and for all. But in killing off the 275 for the Daytona, Ferrari had also killed the magic *mélange* of qualities that made this last run of the first-generation cars so extraordinarily fine.

To put this, or any other, Ferrari, in proper perspective, however, we have to go back to the between-the-wars period when Enzo Ferrari was first honing the rare combination of talents that have given him and his cars a unique place in motoring history.

Most of the men who built up and ran car manufacturing companies, large or small, were first and foremost businessmen. Given an entrepreneurial streak, they perceived the huge market that cars would command and decided to do something about it, either by converting their existing light industrial manufacturing enterprises to vehicle production or by starting from scratch.

Enthusiasts they were not. There have been plenty of enthusiast car makers, of course, and a long list of them can be found at any bankruptcy official's office. But that did not matter, as the motivation of entrepreneurs was the altogether more manageable one of simply wanting to get rich. Neither were they engineers, in the main. But that didn't matter, either: engineers can be hired. Similarly, salesman are available. And so are people with all the other specialist skills needed to design, develop and profitably produce a car.

As it first appeared in 1964, the original 275 with radially spoked alloy wheels. The rear name badge soon moved up to the boot lid and was at least easier to clean there: the GTB's aerodynamics draw a film of oil and muck from the exhaust onto the vertical rear panel

Enzo Ferrari, however, was different, to say the least of it. He came out of a much finer mould altogether. His biography has been too well and extensively recorded elsewhere to need repetition here. But it is important in assessing any of his cars to know at least something of the man. An unenthusiastic scholar, any chance he might have had of training as an engineer was eliminated by the First World War. Ferrari came home from that war bent on getting into motor racing, though he had to start humbly enough as a test driver of road cars before graduating to racing and a not very distinguished career—success in the Targa Florio apart—with Alfa Romeo. He remained closely involved with Alfa, and when that company decided to take one step back from direct participation in motor sport, Ferrari, whose career as a driver clearly was not going to make much more progress, came into his own. He became the entrepreneur who took over the Alfa team and ran it, at one remove, on behalf of the factory.

It's a system that's been used many times since by other large manufacturers: the business of maintaining the team is freed from head office bureaucracy and handed over to an independent who has every incentive to keep costs down and results up if he wants to stay in the job. If the team wins it's a success for Alfa Romeo (or whoever). If it loses, well, what can you expect of a privately run effort?

Managing the Alfa team in this way, however, was something that Ferrari did brilliantly. His talents are many and various, and nearly all of them came to the fore in this new role. The opportunist in him spotted the possibilities of Scuderia Ferrari in the first place; the entrepreneur put the deal together, helped by his ability at corporate politicking; the engineer saw

how the cars should be developed to stay competitive; and skill in the selection of the right personnel—there's no single word in English, unfortunately, for this almost Olympian ability to perceive, judge, and then play off against one another the various human qualities—enabled him to bring together the right group of people to get the job done.

More or less the same very rare mixture of strengths clearly motivated Bugatti, although he was demonstrably more of an artist—and less of a businessman—than Ferrari. The only possible British counterparts who come to mind, and neither Bugattistes nor Ferraristi will probably thank me for daring to mention them in the same breath as their own high priests, are Sir William Lyons (of Jaguar) and Colin Chapman (of Lotus). Of these, though, only Chapman shares the most basic motivation of all that impelled Ferrari—the love of motor racing.

And, as Colin Chapman was to do in the 1960s,

Seen between tests at the Modena Autodrome, this short-nose 275 exemplifies the relatively bluff front end that promoted aerodynamic lift at high speed

Ferrari went into business as a road car manufacturer in the postwar days primarily as a means of generating enough money to go racing properly.

As Italy picked itself up from the havoc and rubble of the war it was obvious that while motor racing, at least on an amateur level, might get started again soon—Italy, after all, being to this sport very much what Rome is to the Christian Church—it was obvious that Ferrari would have to start from scratch.

He did so by setting up as a manufacturer. Now those few words, 'setting up as a manufacturer', cover about as much hard work, worry, anguish, blood, sweat and tears as it's possible to imagine in starting a business.

But ambition and ability carried him through, aided by the fact that Ferrari's native Modena is about the least difficult place on earth in which to start in this particular industry.

The whole area is, and had been for many years, totally in love with the motor car in its finer form: not the mass-produced kind of thing stamped out up the road in Milan by the worker ants of Fiat, but the lovingly hand-crafted work of the master metalsmith that a good Ferrari (or Maserati, Lamborghini, Osca, Stanguellini, Moretti, Volpini, or any one of a dozen other makes from that region) can be.

Ferrari began by supplying cars with which his clients could go racing. This part of the world was (but sadly no longer is) almost equally thickly populated with wealthy aristocrats of a sporting turn of mind for whom car racing—especially on the public road circuits—was as enticing as *almost* any other sport they could imagine.

The engineer in Ferrari had appreciated that—as a rule of thumb of the crudest kind—the most successful competition cars nearly always had six- or eight-cylinder engines. Simple four-cylinder sloggers, often beloved of the British, could never be made to rev high enough to produce adequate power, their main attraction being that they were cheap to make. Ferrari also realised that the car with a six or an eight can be priced a great deal higher than its humble four-cylinder equivalent.

With typical panache, then, and after a brief flirtation with a straight-eight design, Ferrari decided to top all his rivals from the start and go for a 12-cylinder layout. Legend has it that he had been struck by the V12s in a few American luxury cars before the war (with their turbine-like smoothness he could hardly have failed to be impressed). But it should not be forgotten that Britain's W. O. Bentley pointed the way in the V12 he designed for Lagonda in the late 1930s.

We'll be taking a much closer look at the classic Ferrari V12 later on in this book. But it's just worth putting on record here—and this is no criticism of the man—that Ferrari has never been an innovator in automotive engineering. His strength in this area has lain in the ability to select the best ideas of others and then hone, develop and fine-tune them until—when done by Ferrari—they are the best, full stop.

Ferraris for the street set the standard, in terms of performance and roadholding, by which any other sporting car is measured.

For this writer's money, at least, Ferrari *is* motor racing. A Grand Prix without the Ferrari team is not a real Formula 1 race at all. And Le Mans has not been *Le Mans* since Ferrari stopped taking a serious interest in sports car racing. No one, not the calculating engineers at Porsche or the shrewd, innovative Colin Chapman, can begin to compare with the stature of Ferrari in motor sport.

*The original GTB prototype
car, a prime example of
Pininfarina's voluptuous
period in styling*

As these words are written Enzo Ferrari is coming to the end of a long yet not altogether happy life as a demi-god of cars and motor sport.

In his achievements, both as a producer of road cars and a dominating force on the race track, he has far outstripped his only possible rival, Ettore Bugatti.

As a businessman he built up a company that has made him a man of considerable wealth, then ironically underscored his adroit business sense by selling out to a grateful Gianni Agnelli at Fiat at a time when the alternative could well have been collapse.

In private life the story of Ferrari has been less happy, indeed tragic at times. His son Dino, who looked to have inherited his father's engineering and styling talents and perhaps more besides, died in his twenties of leukaemia.

There have been more than a few rumours that Ferrari has other sons, born outside his marriage, including two men occupying senior positions on the racing side at Maranello. But that kind of backstairs gossip, whether true or not, is irrelevant to the story of the cars themselves.

Ferrari himself has lived a relatively austere life in his later years, commuting between a flat in the centre of Modena and the factory out in the hills at Maranello. In recent years much of his time has also been spent at the super-automated Fiorano test track. That is because his professional life has come full circle, ending as it began with a total involvement in racing; machines like the 275 are in the past. Today's Ferrari road car is not really a product of the *Cavaliere* himself but of a group of highly competent designers and marketing men, still intensely Italianate in the motoring sense. Many of them have a Fiat background, for as a company today

Ferrari is effectively the major sporting offshoot of the Fiat group.

So to enjoy a true Ferrari on the road you have to experience one of the pre-Fiat era cars, built when Ferrari was very much the master of all he surveyed, and before the road car business was handed over to Fiat in exchange for financial backing for the racing team. And the finest, and the last, of those pre-Fiat Ferraris is, without doubt, the 275.

For years, while the earlier 250GT short-wheelbase berlinettas and the later Daytonas raced ahead in value, the 275 hung back as a kind of Ferrari 'sleeper', an undervalued model appreciated only by a few. Back in, say, 1974 you could have bought even the pick-of-the-bunch GTB 4-cam for around £4500.

Then they started to take off: some appreciative articles in the press by such connoisseurs of fine cars as Leonard Setright helped spread the word, and suddenly the 275 was 'in' as a desirable Ferrari for the collector. Most of all, the 4-cam went ahead by leaps and bounds, helped in Britain by its extreme rarity: an estimated 27 right-hand-drive examples were imported. It was followed in value by the long-nose, torque-tube single-cam cars, and then at a respectful distance by the earlier GTBs and the GTS convertible. Today, a 4-cam is exceeded in value among Ferrari road cars (albeit by a long way) only by a genuine — as opposed to latter day chop-top — Daytona Spider. The semi-roadgoing alloy-bodied competition 250GT swb is worth more, but was built primarily as a competition car. And the likelihood is that 275s will continue to climb as more collectors come to appreciate their unique place in Ferrari history — and the fact that, 250GTOs apart, they are more satisfying to drive than almost any other 'street' Ferrari.

Chapter 2
The heart of it all– engine

As we have seen, Ferrari's first thoughts on the subject of power units for his earliest car led him towards a straight eight. That was expedient at the time—an eight could be built up borrowing a lot of readily available components since it was in part based on two Fiat 'fours' set end to end. But the problems associated with lengthy in-line engines (like coming up with a suitably stiff crankshaft, not to mention the sheer length of the power unit) meant that a more practical solution was required.

By going to a 60-degree V12 Ferrari at once solved the length problem—for a V12 is not much longer than a six-cylinder in-line engine of half the capacity—while increasing the number of cylinders for more power; using higher crankshaft revolutions without unnecessarily heavy reciprocating parts.

What's more, one suspects, the marketing expert in Ferrari also foresaw the tremendous cachet that would attach to a 12-cylinder car, be it for road or track.

The basic V12, as laid out by design engineer Gioacchino Colombo for Ferrari, was seemingly a power unit of quite splendid complication. Yet in practice it was quite simple—providing you

remember that it was effectively two six-cylinder single overhead camshaft units (and there's nothing complex about that) on a common crankcase.

Designed in the days before pent-roofs, flattened hemispheres and other odd shapes came along to revise European thinking in combustion chamber design, the Ferrari V12 received quite steeply inclined, and therefore large valves, and domed pistons, in most design variants with slots milled out to ensure valve head clearance. Valve operation was by rockers actuated from the centrally located camshaft, so that there was only one broad valve chest per bank. But it presented

Awaiting re-installation in a long-nose, torque tube 275 following overhaul, this single-cam-per-bank 275 engine has the classic Ferrari valve covers in black crackle paint, six twin-choke Webers crammed on top, twin vertical distributors driven off the rear of the camshafts, a capacious wet sump (only the 4-cam cars had dry sump) and the single engine mount on each side. This combined with a single mount per side on the rear-located gearbox to give 4-point location for the entire assembly

There's an engine in there somewhere. A less than pristine 2-cam engine compartment, with mammoth air cleaner shrouding most of the good bits. The twin inlet stacks per side on the air cleaner help control air flow into the main cleaner, which acts as a plenum chamber, to improve throttle response and part-throttle running

lines of shafts for the cams and for the rockers when the cover was removed. The camshafts were chain driven, in the interests of keeping down both production costs and noise level. Gear drive would have been more sophisticated but quite unnecessary for the crankshaft speeds then expected.

Heads and block were sand cast in silumin aluminium alloy, using the traditional Modenese facility for quick and fuss-free casting that has helped distinguish Italian high-performance car manufacture over the years from that in Britain, where most foundries want a minimum order of a zillion units and can promise delivery towards the end of the next decade.

The crankshaft was produced by the best method possible, being machined from a solid billet of steel rather than from a forging or—heaven forbid, although it has sufficed for some remarkably meaty American V8s—from an iron casting.

Carburation was provided by Weber, long favoured by Modena engineers, using three double-choke units from Edoardo Weber's plant in nearby Bologna.

And that in essence was the original Ferrari engine that appeared first in 1946 and stayed in production for over two decades.

It must be said that during its 22-year life span a lot of changes occurred. The capacity grew from 1.5 litres to 3.3 litres, by way of intermediate capacities that included the 3-litre size that made the 250GT and GTO series famous in the mid to late 1950s and on into the early 1960s.

The cylinder heads in particular came in for a lot of revision. The first series-production design used siamesed inlet ports that severely restricted existing breathing, as well as ensuring that the engine could never have a single-carburettor-choke-per-cylinder set-up that is essential for maximum power. Also, Colombo had been less than generous with his head stud arrangements, assuming that three per cylinder would suffice. They did not, as power outputs, bmep and thermal loadings all rose in line with the extraction of more power from the V12.

Some 6-carburettor single-cam cars got these slimmed-down air cleaners that left much more of the magnificent V12 on show

By the late 1950s both problems had been solved on racing versions of the engine by the introduction of an entirely new head design, with separate inlet ports (thus permitting the installation of six twin-choke Webers when required) and four instead of three studs per cylinder. At the same time the spark plug location was moved over to the outside of the heads, improving accessibility as well as giving better ignition.

With the happy facility that Ferrari had in those days for swapping road and racing components around, the new heads soon turned up on production cars.

By 1963, however, even with the revised engine, the 250GT series had been developed about as far as it could go and it was clearly time

At the front, between the oil filler caps, are dual, inverted oil filters. The broad valve covers enclose a central camshaft per bank, operating inclined valves via two lines of shaft-mounted rockers

to start with ... well, not a clean sheet of paper but certainly a new development programme.

The resulting cars, the 275GTB and its derivatives, used the original, classic Ferrari V12 (and we are ignoring here all the many other cylinder configurations tried from time to time by the factory) in its final form.

The cubic capacity had been stretched to the maximum possible, opening out the wet-linered block to give a bore of 77 mm while retaining the 58.8 stroke of the 250 engine, but making it still more oversquare (the V12 having always been advanced in this respect) and obtaining a 10 per cent increase in size to 3285.7 cc.

Power output was quoted at 280 bhp at 7600 rpm for the standard GTB (B for berlinetta)

This parts list illustration shows the way in which the 275, following established Ferrari pattern, had its sohc system arranged. A central camshaft operated rockers with roller cam followers. Rockers were mounted in cast housings that in effect gave two rocker shafts per bank, although in practice each rocker had its own short shaft

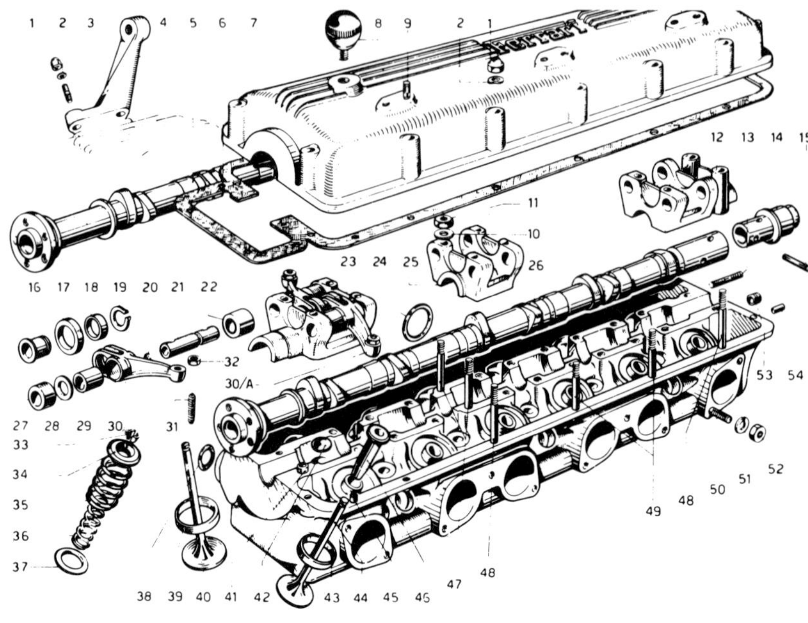

Another parts list drawing, showing a crankshaft machined from a solid billet of steel, the forged piston and the short, meaty con rod

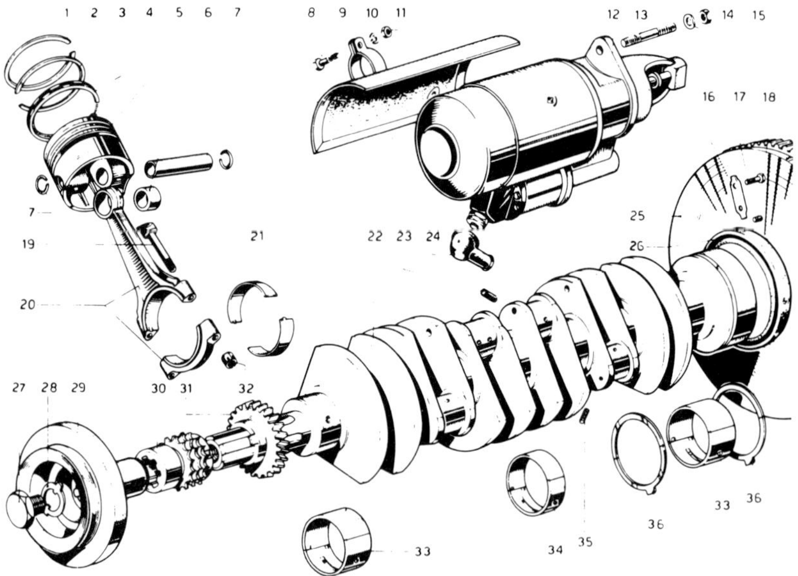

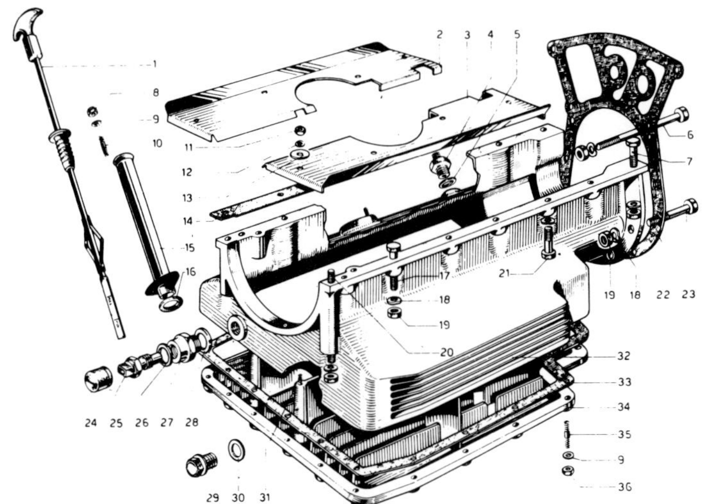

Disliking the cheap, pressed steel kind of sump, Ferrari used yet another alloy casting, heavily ribbed for both strength and cooling, and with sufficient location to add materially to crankcase rigidity. The base, which was detachable, was extensively baffled to prevent oil surge

engine, using three twin-choke Webers. As an optional extra buyers could specify a six carburettor set-up that was claimed to give another 40 bhp at 7500 rpm. Inexplicably, you could have the six-carb option with the GTB coupé, but not if you opted for the GTS (S for spider) convertible, which came only in a milder state of tune at 260 bhp at 7600 rpm. However, rules were made to be broken at Ferrari; at least a few *six*-carb GTSs exist today.

The 275 engine (275, by the way, derives from the individual cylinder capacity in cc—a system of nomenclature long, but not exclusively, adhered to by Ferrari) continued in this form from the introduction of the model in 1964 up to the Paris Show of September 1966. Compared to its rivals the engine, even though a far from new design, still eclipsed that of all rivals bar one. Porsche had yet to venture into the big league, while the around-4-litre in-line sixes of Jaguar and Aston Martin were clumsy by comparison. The only problem was that a few miles along the Autostrada del Sole in Bologna local industrialist Ferruccio Lamborghini was spending a fortune

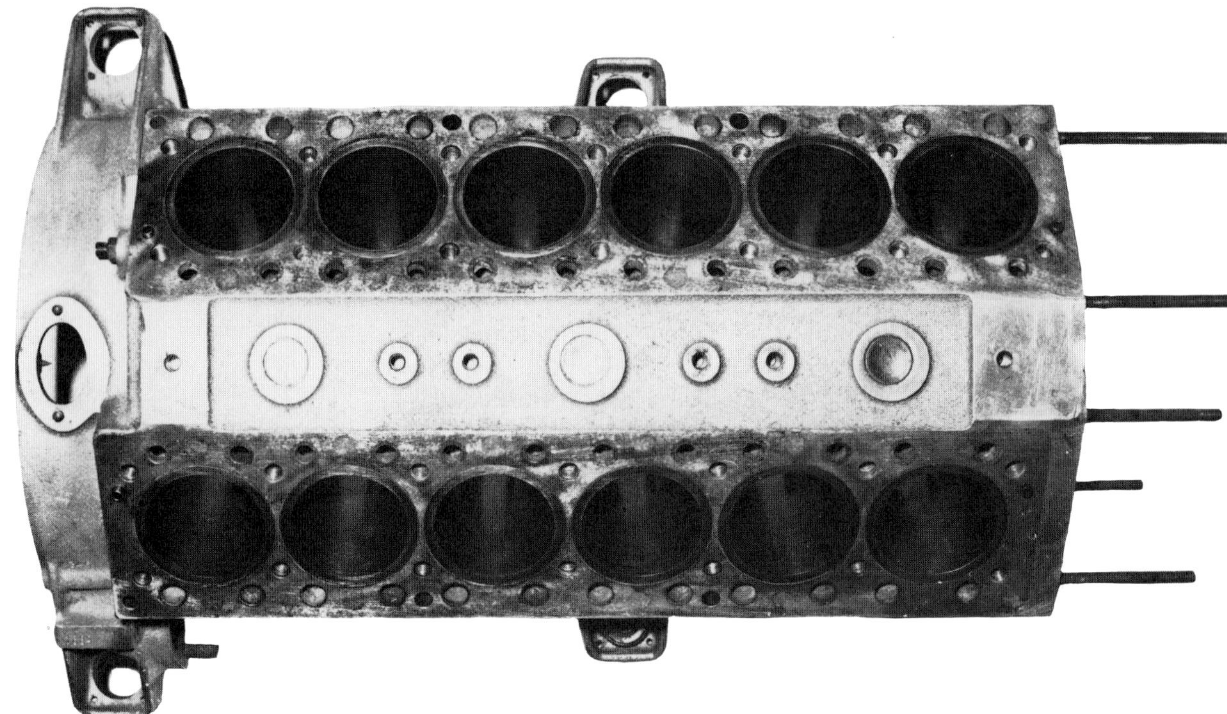

Emphasising just how longlived a good design can be, the 275 block was a development of the original Colombo engine

trying (vainly as it finally transpired) to establish himself as a rival to Ferrari. The Lamborghini engine, too, was a light-alloy V12. But it went one better, technically, than the 275 in boasting two overhead camshafts per bank of cylinders, making an impressive four in all. And there was no doubt that, thus powered, Lamborghini's svelte coupés went like the wind.

Ferrari, though, had the answer at hand—or about as far away as the competitions department's parts bins. Back in 1957 a twin-cam-per-bank version of the basic single-cam-per-bank had been designed for sports car racing. It had worked wonderfully well, only being discarded when sports car competition engine design began to lean more towards pure Grand Prix technology for most manufacturers, while Ferrari was finding that in cars like the Testa Rossa, the GTO and the 250LM the good old sohc design would suffice to get the job done against mediocre opposition.

So there were the super-efficient '4-cam' heads, ready and waiting for the day when they would be needed. And needed they certainly were in 1966 to keep Ferrari abreast, technically, on performance, and in the sales brochure, of what was

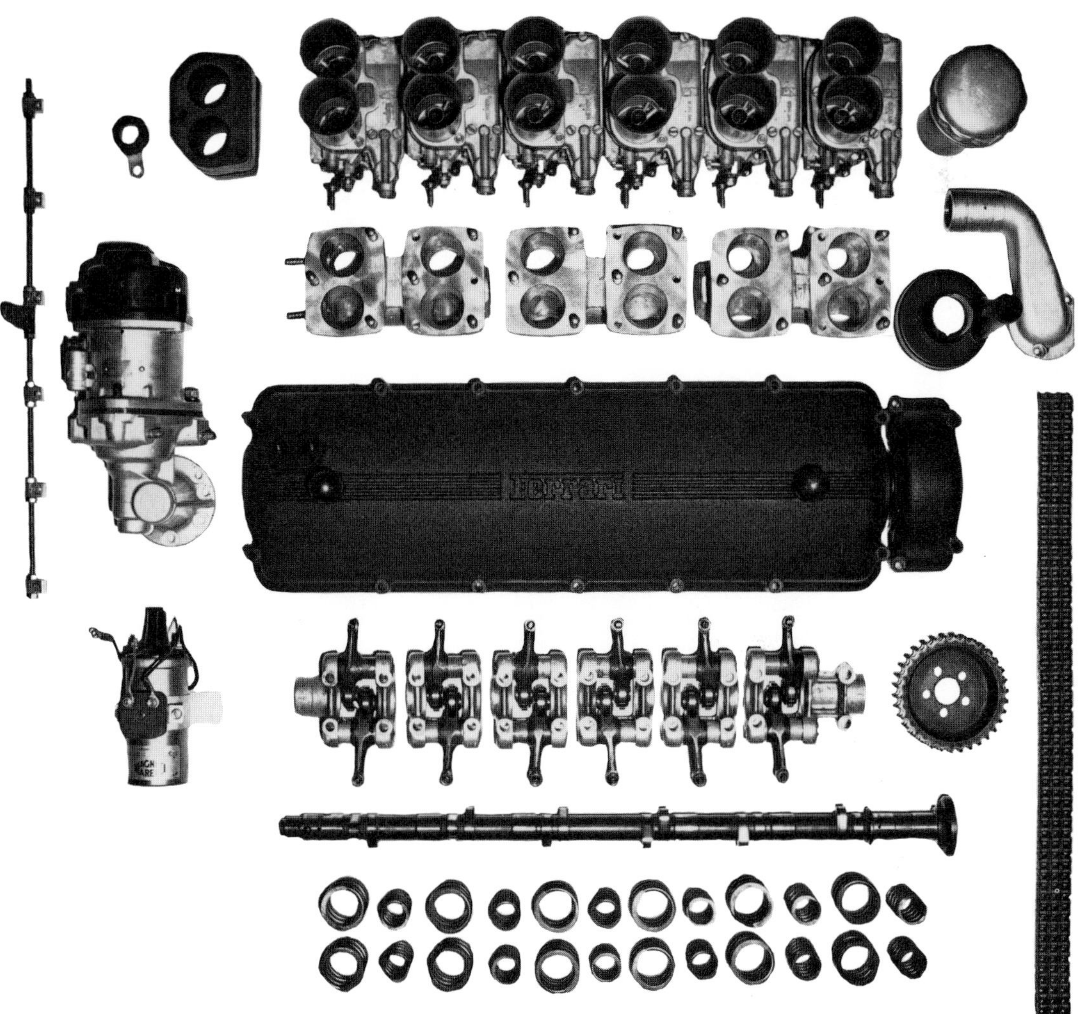

The source of the power: multiple Weber carburettors, plus separate inlet manifolds, above the Ferrari valve cover, roller-follower rockers and a high-profile camshaft below

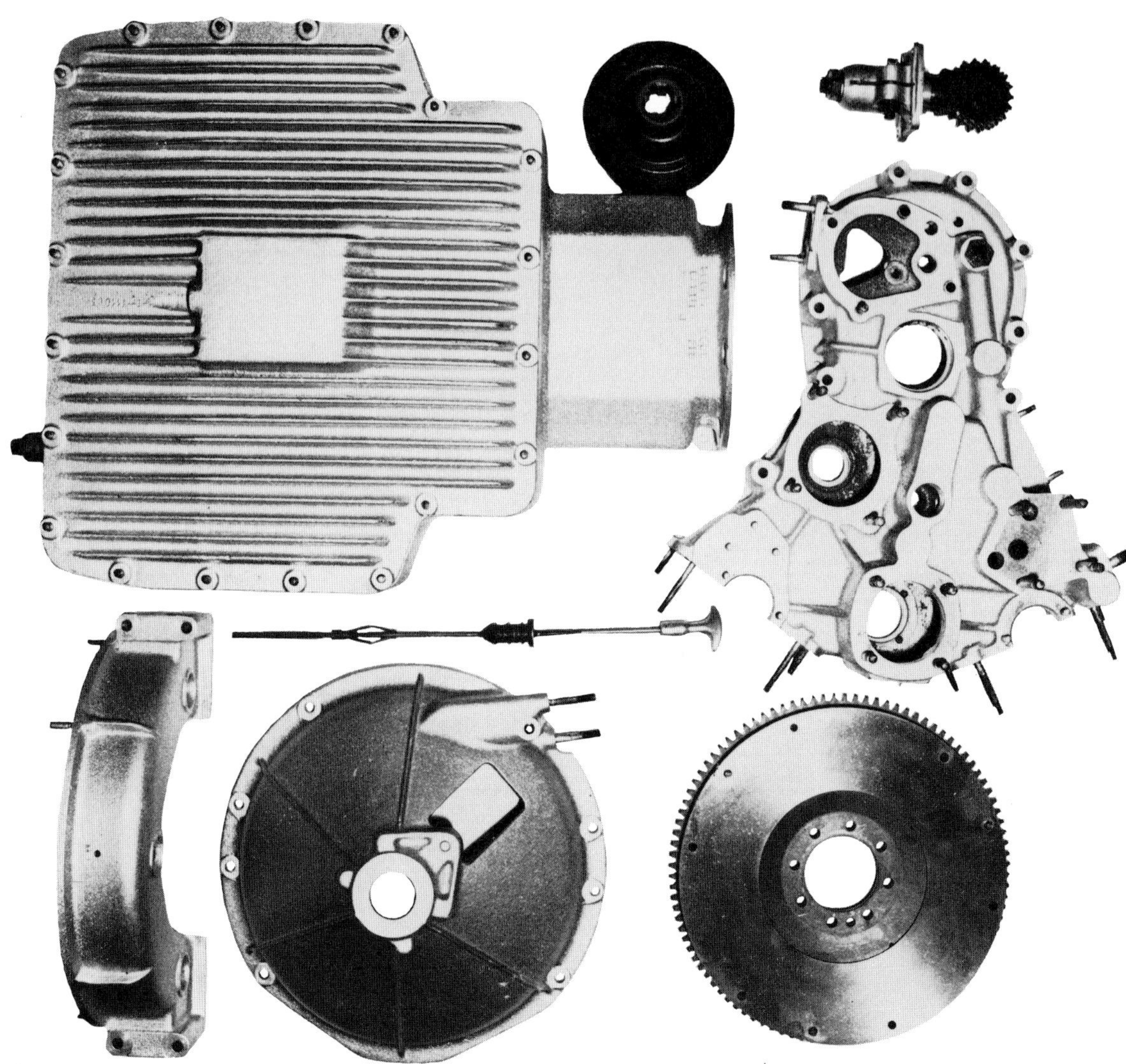

Components that help keep the Ferrari characteristics alive include a slim light flywheel. This is an important factor in instantaneous throttle response and the way in which, with low rotating masses like a racing engine, it dies the second you switch off

coming from Lamborghini. So the sports-racing heads were taken down, dusted off, and with only minor reductions in porting, valve timing, inlet manifold and carburettor size, they were hastily put into production. They bolted almost straight onto the standard block, retaining chain drive for the camshafts as far as the top of the block, with

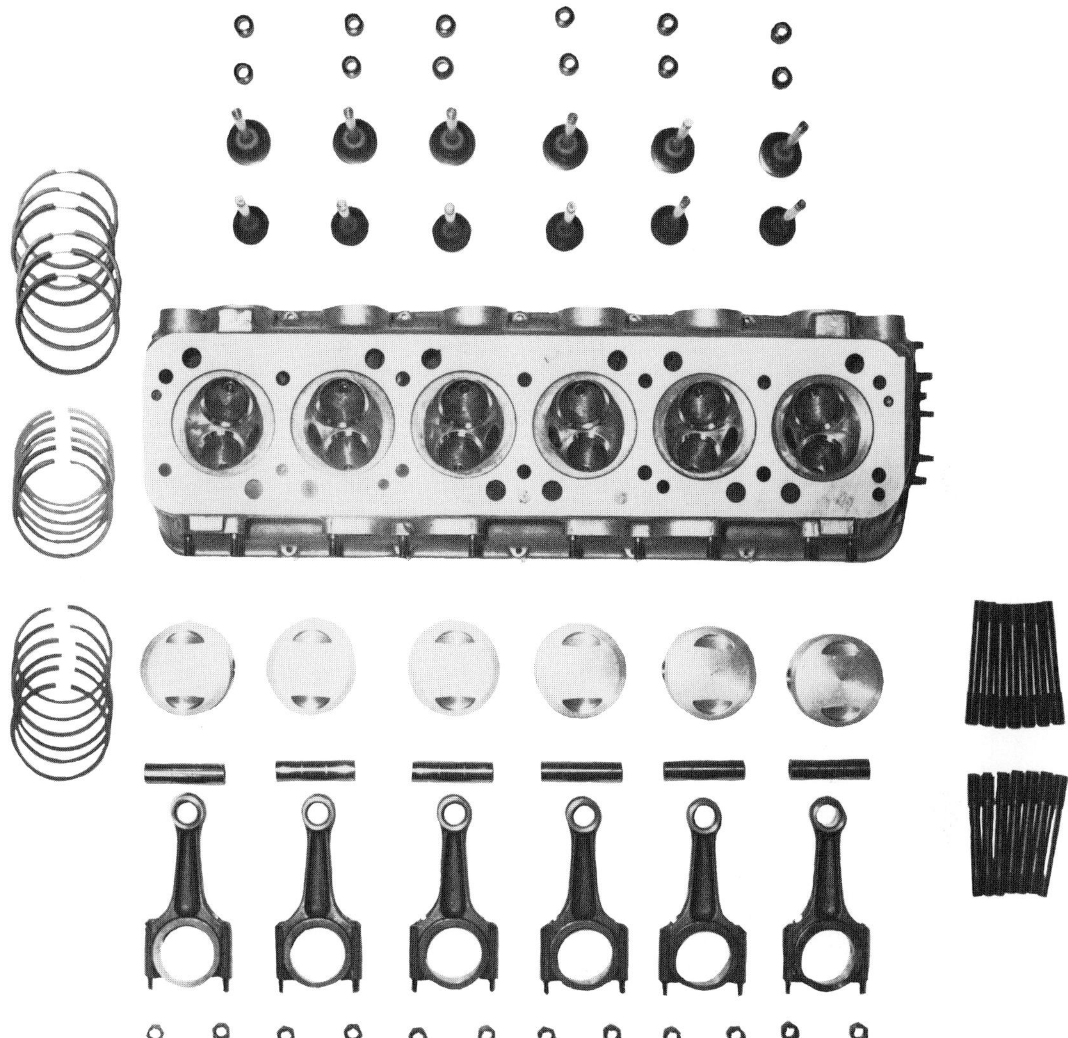

proper racing-style gear drive for the final stage. Six twin-choke Webers were standard.

Thus was the legendary GTB/4 (the 4 indicating 4-cam) born. And to drive, by comparison with a 'single cam' 275, it is as different as chalk and cheese, even if the cheese is as tasty a bit of Bel Paese as is the standard 275.

A 275 combustion chamber is nearly all valve, as this shot of the hemispherical head shows. Piston crowns have slots milled out for valve clearance, and the con rods are prime examples of how to keep reciprocating weight down and strength up

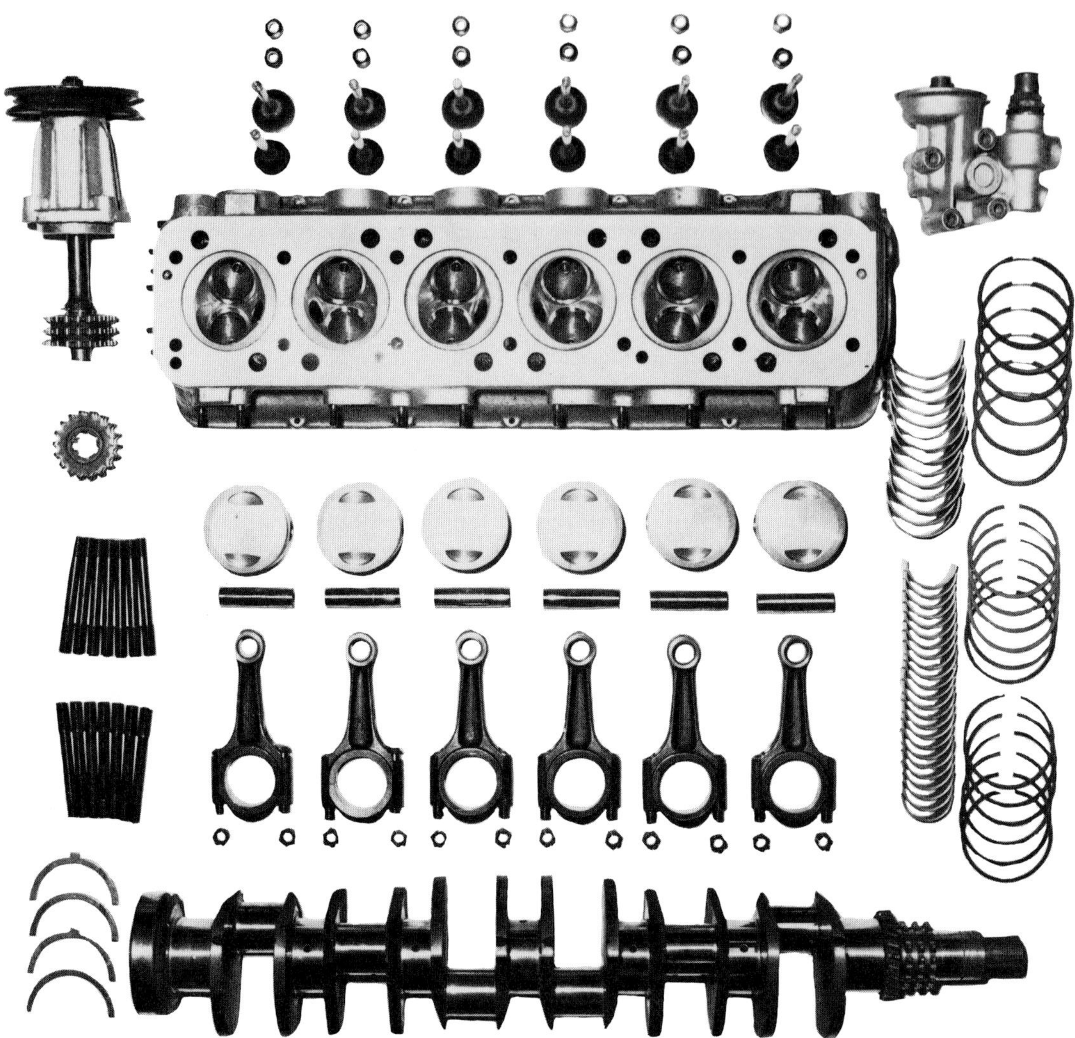

This picture includes the superb crankshaft, machined from the solid, with seven main bearings and six dual-journal big-end bearings, and slender counterweights to minimise reciprocating weight

The cam profile and valve areas on a 4-cam are virtually to racing standards, making the car extraordinarily 'cammy' to drive on the road—and all the more exciting for it. Maintain a delicate foot on the throttle and it will pull quite strongly from as low as 1000 rpm (if you care to mistreat such an engine so), but at around 4000 it suddenly begins to climb onto the cam and at 5500 rpm will howl through the peak torque speed and on in a crescendo of noise and acceleration to a heady 300 bhp at 8000 rpm. Given the right roads—a run across the Cotswolds, say, on a summer dawn—there is no engine so sensually exhilarating to drive behind.

By comparison, the earlier 275s feel almost sedate, although in all honesty they are really very far from that. They have the traditional Ferrari characteristic of ample, smooth power all the way up the rev range—and even an 'ordinary' 275 runs easily to 7000 rpm—without the sudden lurch of low-down torque but top-end breathlessness one associates with an American V8, or the inability to rev that beset most British twin-cam

Looking as though it had just completed a Targa Florio, Nürburgring 1000 km and Le Mans in succession, without much maintenance in between this 3-carburettor, 2-cam engine has rare curved ram pipes. They were so arranged to obtain the length needed for good mid-range torque while maintaining bonnet clearance

The last and the best: the legendary 4-cam engine (minus distributor caps in this shot), a very close relative of Ferrari racing power units

sixes. And the earlier 275s, in particular, are delightfully tractable; quite—well, nearly—as willing to trickle through traffic as Aunty's Morris Minor.

A further shortcoming with these 4-cam heads is that the abrupt, high-lift cam lobes and heavy-duty valve springs give the valve actuation

system a hard life, especially if it is allowed to idle for any length of time. The valve stem is surmounted by an inverted bucket-type follower, in the customary ohc way, and the cam lobe bears on that. Valve clearance is obtained by inserting the requisite thickness of shim in a recess on the top of the follower, and it is this shim in fact that is

With no air cleaner, the twin-cam-per-bank GTB/4 engine can be seen to advantage. In the top right hand corner, next to the battery, is the filler for the dry sump oil tank. Battery and tank are moved to the left on rhd 4-cam cars

At least one GTB/4 acquired air conditioning, with the pump tucked away at the front of the engine

in direct contact with the cam. The same system is used on Fiat's 125/132 or Lancia Beta twin-cam cylinder head (indeed, the shims are interchangeable between the Ferrari and its more homely compatriots) and they wear at a phenomenal rate in the 275 unless clearances are checked regularly. In short order the wear can spread to the cam lobes too, leaving a careless owner with, at best, a bill for four new camshafts. At worst, the worn shim spreads out in the cam follower guide, either jamming the follower or leading to its collapse with ensuing expensive valve-to-piston intimacy. The secret of a reliable Ferrari is eternal vigilance; constant, painstaking maintenance.

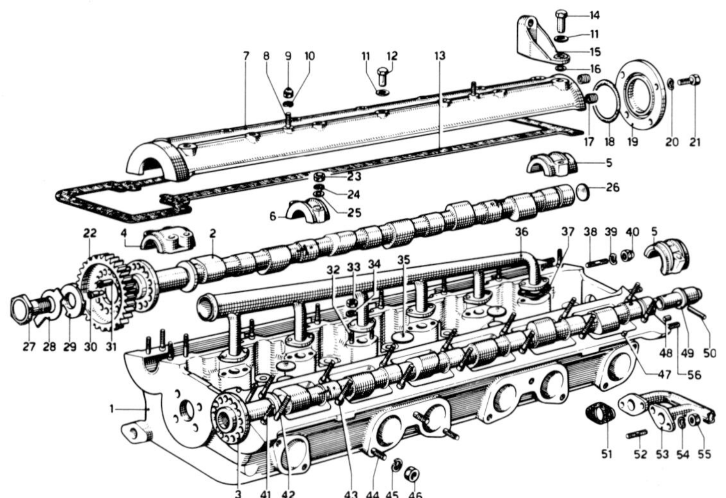

Despite apparent complexity, the 4-cam head is really quite simple with two gear-driven camshafts (the primary drive to the top of the block being by chain, still) and a central water manifold

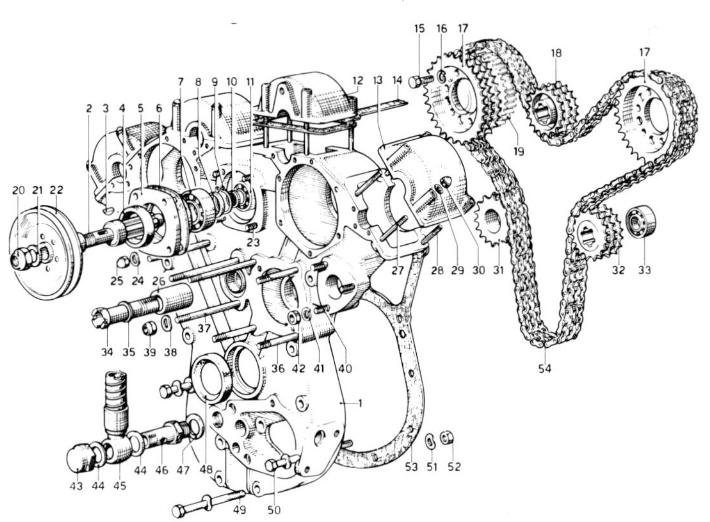

This parts list picture shows the timing cover of the 4-cam, with the primary drive by chain from the crankshaft to the gear-driven camshafts

Given that they can be quite reasonably trouble-free.

The 4-cam is no lover of traffic, unfortunately. While, if properly maintained, it should suffer from little or no plug fouling, it definitely does not take kindly to low speeds, the superb throttle response making it all the more sensitive under those conditions. And water temperatures rise easily. That is cured by a rather Heath Robinson arrangement of cooling fans (two 3-blade devices driven by re-worked Lucas wiper motors!), but then general under-bonnet temperatures soon rise to the point at which vapour lock starts. Anticipating this, the handbook tells you to switch on the electric auxiliary fuel pump, which is normally there only to prime the carburettors in the morning before starting. Meanwhile, torrents of warm air pour out of the four engine compartment vents just ahead of the scuttle on either side. If only they had put one or two vents in the top, where they're needed. . . .

Oil temperature, on the other hand, is less of a problem. When adopting full-race heads for the final 275, Ferrari went the whole hog and installed a racing dry-sump oil system as well. Over four gallons of oil are circulated through a tank mounted in the wing, and this provides enough cooling on most cars to make an oil radiator unnecessary. One or two of the early 4-cams had a zig zag gilled tube affair snaking across the front of the water radiator and looking like nothing so much as a leftover from one of those giant Edwardian racing cars. But this never seems to have got into production.

Even in single-cam form, with broad black-crackle valve covers topping either head and a row of Webers down the middle, the Ferrari engine is a good-looking unit.

In 4-cam form, with twin valve chests per bank

and six carburettors it's a particularly elegant and impressive engine. So it's unfortunate that much of the machinery is covered by a vast air cleaner. You *can* remove it, and Weber *can* supply bell-mouth ram pipes that set off the engine to perfection. But, especially on the 4-cam, the carburation system needs the air-cleaner to help align the air flow. Without it, even the best technician can spend days jetting and re-jetting the Webers to give clean running throughout the rev range yet still fail to reach the perfect throttle response that is available with that dreary air cleaner in place.

One of the qualities that distinguishes a purpose-built high-performance engine, a thoroughbred like the Ferrari, from basically humble units which have attained power by post-production modification is this response and throttle running.

All 275 engines—even the wild, near-race 4-cam—will pull smoothly and accelerate strongly from very low revs, running cleanly on a near-closed throttle and responding instantaneously to demands for increased power. At least they will if the driver treats them properly.

By contrast, a highly tuned Chevrolet or Ford, say, tends to stumble and misfire on part-throttle no matter how skilful the driver. Until they are running at or near full bore they feel—indeed, are—overcarburated and difficult to get up on the cam.

Once the last 4-cams were made the era was over. The replacement was the Daytona, a massive car in every sense and with the kind of monumental acceleration—indeed, there has never been a faster production car—that left even a 275GTB/4 behind. But the Daytona with its excess, not to say excessive, performance, never recaptured the finesse of the 275s.

Chapter 3
The legs on the rest – transmission

The heart of any Ferrari is the engine, but a not too distant second to it in the esteem of any Italian automotive engineer comes the gearbox.

Before the era of the 275, Ferrari had rather belied this belief, at least where the road cars were concerned, by fitting an undistinguished four-speed unit with some readily beatable synchromesh.

But at least Ferrari's boxes were just that: made by the factory. By comparison most rivals, notably Jaguar, were quite content to buy in transmissions, Jaguar favouring the truck-like Moss gearbox until it was at last replaced by one of their own making.

When the need was felt at Ferrari for a five-speed unit on some of the last 250s, the first, quick expedient was to follow the foreign competition and buy in something from a specialist—in this case the Laycock de Normanville overdrive, an electrically selected and disengaged overdrive ratio in a housing that could be mounted on an existing transmission casing.

The next step, though, had to be a proper five-speeder: not only had the concept of having two gear levers (one for the box, the other a flick-switch for the overdrive) proved unacceptable to customers but the overdrive worked out none too well in practice on the 250, partly as a result of lubrication problems.

Now Ferrari already made some beautiful five-speed gearboxes for the sports-racing cars. But these were unsuitable for the road. They lacked synchromesh and only a properly competent driver—and by no means all Ferrari customers were necessarily that—could cope. So when the later 330GT models got their five-speed boxes it was in the form of a heavy unit, almost ponderous by Ferrari standards; of course it did, at least, boast synchromesh.

For the 275, it seemed, something better was in order. Advantage could be taken of the opportunity to put the gearbox at the rear of the car in the interests of better weight distribution, helping the 275 to get nearer a 50/50 balance. That was no bad idea. Most Ferraris, indeed most front-engined cars of any make, obviously have a preponderance of weight over the front wheels that increases the tendency to understeer. By removing the gearbox from its customary position and mating it with the differential instead, a considerable weight could be moved several feet farther back in the chassis, with consequent benefit to handling. The decision proved a particularly wise one in the case of the 275s, which have their engines mounted well forward and certainly much closer to the front axle line than was the case in the earlier 250s.

As with most Ferrari features, the idea was not new. It was just that Ferrari and his engineers could again take the best ideas of the others, develop them and perfect them so that in time Ferrari people came almost to seem like the originators. In the case of the rear-mounted gearbox, Ferrari himself had been well enough exposed to the idea elsewhere, had used the scheme himself—as had Maserati—for competition cars and had seen Lancia utilise it for some production models.

Clearly, the rear-mounted gearbox only worked if the car which was to receive it had either de Dion rear suspension or, like the 275, an independent rear end, calling for a chassis-mounted differential unit to which the gearbox itself could be mounted.

The first 275s located the engine four-square on cast lugs projecting from the corners of the block, and took the drive back from the conventionally placed clutch to the gearbox by means of a long and slender shaft. This prop shaft, running at engine speed instead of road speed, had no universal joints. But it was designed to be whippy enough to accommodate minor misalignments between engine and gearbox. To prevent it getting altogether too flexible, however, and whirling like a skipping rope, the shaft was steadied halfway along its length by a chassis-mounted bearing.

The first run of 275s used a slender shaft with a central steady-bearing to take the drive back to the rear-mounted transaxle unit. On later cars a rigid tube enclosed the shaft and made the entire package into a single, elongated unit of engine, gearbox and final drive

Inevitably (as one can say with hindsight) there was some conflict in the component parts of this assembly. All too often under torque reaction or *g* forces the engine and gearbox would go out of line, loading up the centre bearing of the prop shaft and producing all manner of odd vibrations. Bearings wore out quickly and were difficult—and therefore expensive—to replace. As an interim measure some cars received constant velocity joints at each end of the shaft.

The cure for the problem, introduced with the second series 275s, the long-nose models, was to connect the engine and gearbox rigidly by means of a torque tube. This eliminated all the prop shaft difficulties at a stroke, made the whole car slightly quieter and allegedly improved the handling by stiffening up the chassis. However, with all due respect to 275 aficionados who subscribe to this claim, it is hard to see how the engine/torque-tube/gearbox/differential package, one long and rigid structure as it then became, could really contribute anything noticeable to the rigidity of a chassis frame to which it was attached by rubber mountings.

In introducing the torque tube, which was also adapted for the larger 330/365GTC series, Ferrari revised the engine mounts themselves. The engine was now supported by a single mount on either side of the block only, with a similar single mount per side at the transaxle, thus giving four-point location for the entire assembly.

Like a handful of other no-expense-spared sports and GT cars of the era, the 275 had racing-style ball-bearing spline articulated drive shafts. The low-friction bearings in the splines ensured that the shafts did not lock solid under heavy acceleration while the car was heeled over on a bend. Conventional drive shafts tend to lock up under these conditions, momentarily losing their

With the engine liable to move in one direction at one end, and the transaxle at the other, the open propshaft of early cars—having no UJs—had a hard time of it. This central steady bearing used to wear out regularly and was tricky to replace

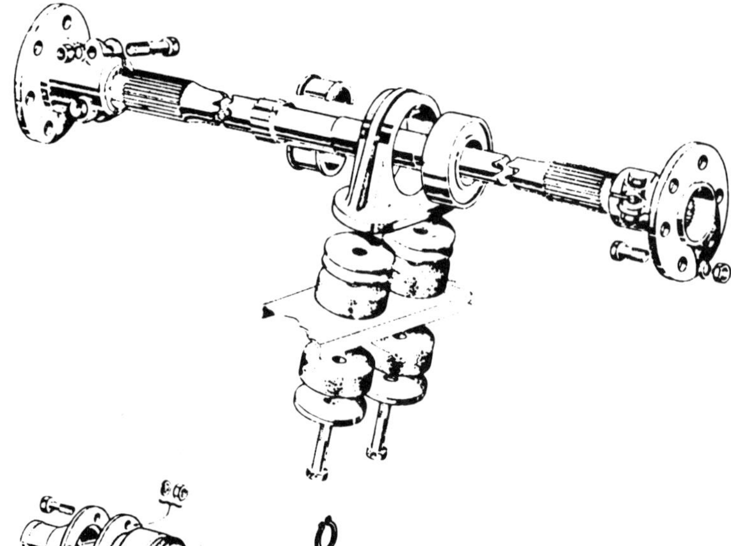

Things got better later when constant velocity joints were added at each end of the shaft

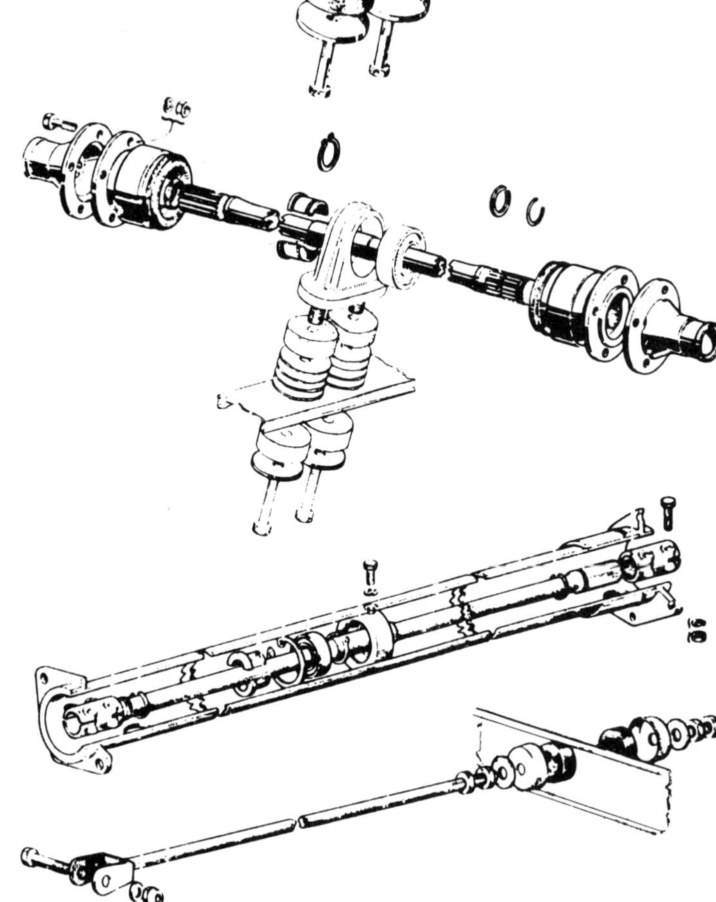

The final answer, though, was to tie everything up inside a rigid tube that prevented relative movement and permitted a return to solid couplings at each end

ability to telescope and thereby making the rear suspension solid, with resultant—and unsought— oversteer. Nine drivers out of 10 probably never pushed their 275s hard enough to appreciate this refinement. But it's nice to know it's there— another example of Ferrari's providing the sort of car you *needed*, which may or may not have been quite the car you thought you wanted.

The gearchange action is much more positive than you might imagine, given that lever and box are some way apart. Quite a long lever is very accurately located, however, in a cast housing, moving through a proper gate. A single rod, with provision built in for adjustment, runs straight back to enter the forward end of the gearbox itself. So gearchanges called for longer movement than you might expect (especially on right-hand-drive-cars, which have the gear lever still on the left of the transmission tunnel), but are light and positive; precise but not too quick. First is around the corner, in the 'dog leg' position opposite reverse, with 2-3-4-5 occupying the four corners of the main part of the gate.

The synchro is nearly unbeatable with the box warmed through. But a gentle hand and, preferably, double declutching are needed for the first few miles. Until the oil is well warmed some boxes are very reluctant to engage second and it's best not to force the issue but to go straight to third.

The gearbox itself is a perfectly straightforward five-speed, making use of Dr Porsche's excellent synchromesh system and with all indirect ratios. Fifth is geared to around 1:1 (the exact ratio varies in the different 275 models) for quite long-legged cruising, but not so high as to be anything other than a practical top gear. That is, the car is geared to reach peak revs in this ratio.

Chapter 4
2-cam performance; then the 4-cam!

Just what peak revs in top gear means in terms of top speed is no simple matter. Maximum depends on so much—the state of tune of the engine, weather conditions and so on—that even the technical magazines' average from two-way runs is by no means a definitive figure for anything other than that particular car on that particular day. Undoubtedly the figure to aim for when the 275 came along, though, was the 150 mph that *Autocar* and *Motor* had established as a maximum for the rival Jaguar E type. The fact that an E type needed racing tyres and a decidedly crisp, not to say well-tweaked, engine to achieve that was played down. In reality, a true E type figure in those days was probably around 140-145 mph. In the same way, an early GTB would probably manage 145, or possibly 150 mph, with perhaps another 5–10 mph for the six-carburettor version and that much less for the milder, less aerodynamic GTS. The later GTBs with their slimmer, more penetrating noses obviously gained a few mph on the maximum. And the advent of the GTB/4 added a few more mph still. Most important, they *felt* extremely fast, and the generally very accurate speedos did nothing to dispel this impression.

Ignoring possible speedo error, though, and relying on a recently recalibrated rev counter, the author's 4-cam has been known to see 7500 rpm in 5th gear on a suitable flat stretch of road and a still day; with gearing of 22 mph per 1000 rpm in top that equates to 165 mph. Whether that velocity could immediately have been repeated, in best magazine style, by another run in the opposite direction, it has never seemed politic to discover.

More impressive than any outright maximum, anyway, is acceleration and this the 275—

If Henry Ford II had had his way this would have been no joke. Around the time the 275 was in the design stage Ford tried to take over Ferrari as a means to achieving overnight the high performance image sought by the marketing men in Dearborn, Ferrari spurned the American advances, and Ford decided to go it alone with cars like the GT40 and engines like the Cosworth-Ford Grand Prix V8

This Speciale *turned up at some of the 1965 European motor shows. Pininfarina gave it a power bulge on the bonnet, his PF badge by the front wheel arch (production cars had only the horizontal Pininfarina nameplate), and deleted the quarterlight*

particularly the later cars—has in very ample measure up to around 130 mph, at which point aerodynamics begin to play an increasingly large part. Even the next 20 mph come up quickly in a 4-cam, correspondingly less so in the earlier cars.

Getting away from rest is none too easy, thanks to the grip. This makes it difficult to break traction in a racing start without a real risk of breaking something altogether more expensive.

Few road test reports on the 275 have appeared, other than rather general road impressions pieces, due to the factory's notorious lack of interest in those days—shared by most of their overseas agents—in providing cars for harsh and possibly critical treatment at the hands of motoring journalists.

Autosport did manage to road-test a six-carb short-nose GTB, staffman Patrick McNally having overcome Maranello Concessionaires' road-test reticence by buying the car—although not just for the test, one hopes.

McNally timed his GTB at 159 mph as a two-way average, with a top one-way speed of 160.5 mph. 0–60 mph took 6.4 seconds, 0–100 12.5 and the standing kilometre 23.8 seconds with a top speed of 134.5 mph. The standing kilometre performance comfortably beats that of a similar-capacity sports-racing car of just a few years earlier. Then again, McNally's car was one of a handful of lightweights built in 1965 for events like the Tour de France, with aluminium bodywork and—like all competition or semi-competition GTBs—extra air vents in the rear wings.

Fuel consumption averaged 10–13 mpg. Another of these cars was owned by John Dabbs of Northdown Racing, the historic car specialists. He recalls it as being extremely fast. 'The trouble was, though, that you couldn't stop the damn thing.'

A British registered long-nose, 2-cam car with one of the Plexiglas-hooded headlights in its customary condition: misted up

Bereft of bumpers, and with its Borrani competition wheels and racing-style external but recessed filler cap, the GTB looks more like a GTO than ever in this semi-competition form

These 275s had a vast 30-gallon fuel tank that started just behind the seats, as opposed to the smaller single tanks of early standard GTBs and the twin units, totalling 19.8 gallons, fibreglass-covered and mounted in the rear wings, of the later cars.

Another alloy-bodied short-nose 275 was tested by *Sports Car Graphic*. Its weight advantage—dry weight being around 2400 lb against 2500 lb approximately for a steel version—was counteracted by the fact that it had the stock three-carburettor engine. Nonetheless, a top speed of 153 mph was recorded, with a one-way best of 156 mph. 0–60 mph took six seconds, 0–100 14.6 seconds and the standing quarter mile 14 seconds (reaching 98 mph), with 25.4 seconds for the

standing kilometre. It's worth noting that the speedo was calibrated and found to be only one per cent optimistic at 90 mph.

The acceleration times recorded in these and the tests that follow underline the fact that a 275 is a hard car to get off the line fast. The ample weight over the rear wheels, broad tyres, limited slip differential, a high 1st gear and independent rear suspension give superb adhesion making it hard to achieve the nicely controlled wheelspin essential to a quick getaway.

In America, *Automobile Quarterly* borrowed a mildly tweaked 275GTB/4—it had racing 40 DCN-9 Webers on open ram pipes instead of the standard 40 DCN-17s plus air-cleaner—and reported speeds in the gears of 52, 75, 101, 127 and 166

With craftsmen shaping each panel by hand, it's no surprise that no two 275s are quite identical. This late-model 2-cam has a fuller roof and lower front wing line than many of its brothers

Removing the rear bumpers from this GTB/4 has had a marked visual effect in making the car look shorter and heavier from the rear. The protection they offer is so slight that the owner probably felt he had little to lose: even a fairly light tap drives the bumper straight into the panel it is supposed to protect

mph respectively, with 0–100 mph in 15 seconds.

Road & Track managed to get its editorial hands on a 275 NART Spider, also with more power than standard: 330 bhp was spoken of, with similar carburettor changes to the *Automobile Quarterly* car. This example had recently completed the Sebring 12 Hours, finishing a praiseworthy seventeenth overall in the ladylike hands of Denise McCluggage and Pinky Rollo. On test, the Spider managed a 155 mph top speed and a 14.7 second standing quarter mile.

Fuel consumption figures have ranged from 10 mpg under arduous conditions—hard driving on slow roads, or crawling through city traffic—on the various models up to around 17 mpg, which

even a 4-cam can manage on long open-road runs while putting up 70 mph plus point-to-point averages.

Road testers of the day generally considered it impolitic to say anything rude about the brakes. McNally in *Autosport* could afford to be critical, since it was his own car, and he remarked that 'I think the car deserves larger discs and a more powerful servo.' The men from *Automobile Quarterly* surmised at a braking fault in their test 4-cammer. The wrong pads? Air in the hydraulics? They could only guess, not knowing the real cause of the trouble. Other road test writers forbore to mention the brakes at all.

Front view of the same Swiss-owned car, on 7-inch rimmed Borranis. Recessed into the nose is the customary Ferrari prancing horse badge on its rectangular yellow background

Extra Ferrari insignia, other than the standard badging, detract from the car's originality. A few owners have even tried the big shields, with black prancing horse and SF (for Scuderia Ferrari) as stick-on badges for the scuttle. The factory applied these only to its own team cars

What is this car? Usually reliable photographic sources in Italy have called this a 4-cammer with the latest cast wheels. 4-cammers always have a power bulge, or is this something special? Certainly it was photographed in Pininfarina's usual location

Chapter 5
The simple skeleton–chassis

As a generalisation, Britain has always been the home of good chassis design and Italy the heartland of engine excellence.

To most British designers the engine has often seemed almost a burden, to be accommodated as best as possible in one's chassis—nuisance as it is, that great lump of iron taking up half one end of the car. In Italy, the view has traditionally been that the chassis is no more than a necessary evil, there to stop the beautiful engine dragging along the ground.

Certainly Ferrari and his designers took that stance in the early years. As we have seen, their V12 was among the best automotive power units ever produced. The chassis, on the other hand, was distinctly homely. Until the advent of the 275 it had been no more than a tubular, cross-braced ladder affair for the road cars, with double wishbone front end and a live rear axle on semi-elliptic leaf springs, with trailing arms to relieve the springs of most—although by no means all—of the work of locating the axle.

Admittedly, by the days of the last 250s this arrangement had been made to work quite well. Cars like the short-wheelbase berlinetta, the 250GT Lusso and obviously the GTO had excel-

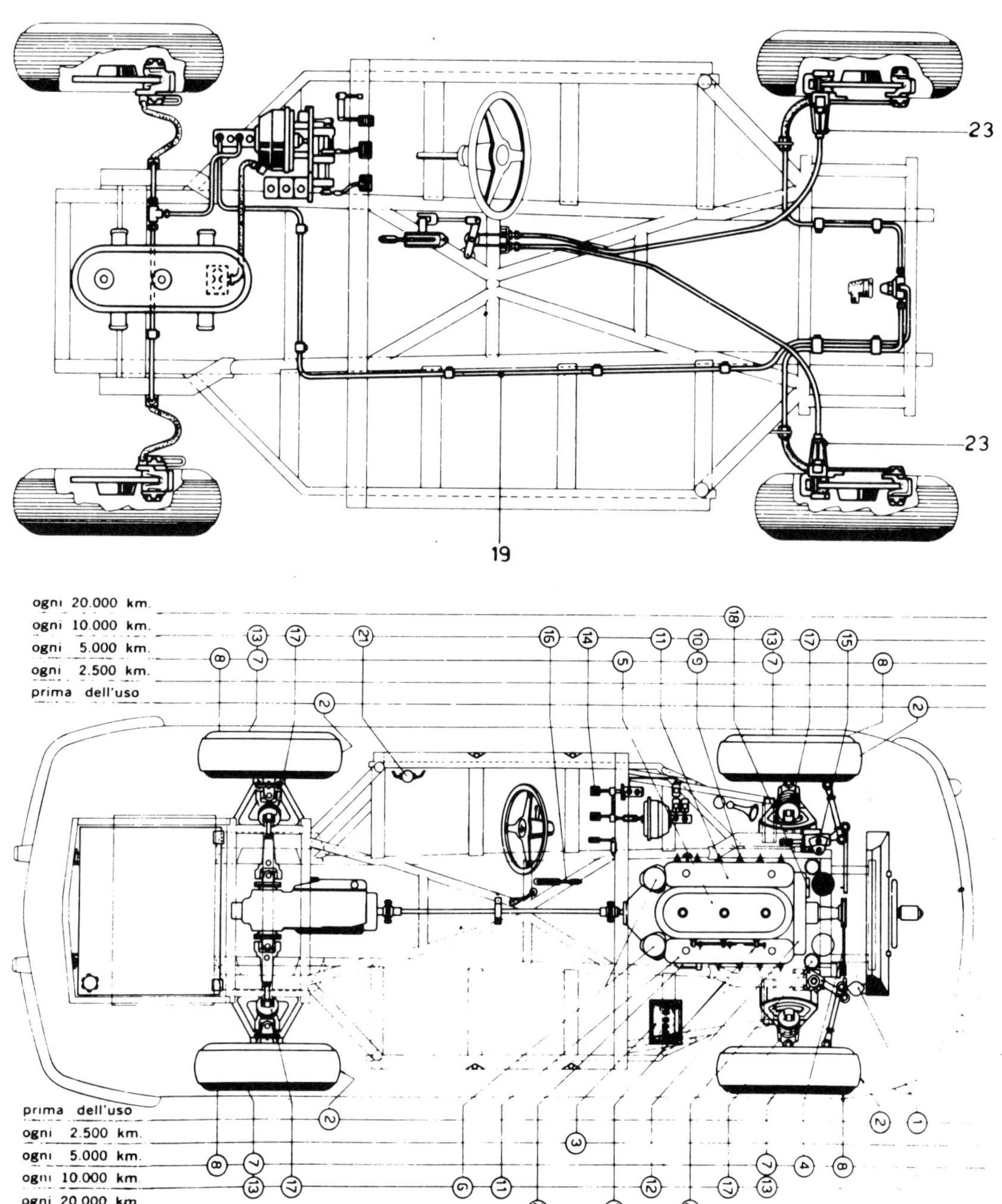
23
19
23
ogni 20.000 km.
ogni 10.000 km.
ogni 5.000 km.
ogni 2.500 km.
prima dell'uso
prima dell'uso
ogni 2.500 km.
ogni 5.000 km.
ogni 10.000 km.
ogni 20.000 km.

lent cornering power and manageable, predictable handling qualities. But they represented the wishbone front/semi-elliptic rear design developed about as far as it would go. For the 275 something more sophisticated was needed, particularly since the rival E type Jaguar had an elegant and effective form of independent rear suspension, besides which the Ferrari's specification in this department looked decidedly outdated.

Fortuitously, the engineers had—as was so often the case at Maranello in those days—to do no more than wander across to the competitions department to find what they needed. Having

62

wrung the last drop of development out of the live rear axle in the legendary 250GTO, Ferrari had gone rear-engined for GT racing with the 250LM. Perforce, this car had independent rear suspension, and that in turn had been developed from the irs set-up first tried on works *front*-engined Testa Rossa sports-racers around 1960.

What worked well in the Testa Rossa and the 250LM would clearly form the basis of a good back end for the next generation of road cars. And, happily for both Ferrari's own fortunes and the driving pleasure of his customers, just the man was on hand to effect the development. This chassis specialist (Ferrari's first ever, cynics might say) was an Englishman, Michael Parkes, who had first come to Enzo Ferrari's notice driving GTOs for British Farrari importer Colonel Ronnie Hoare. But long before he graduated to Ferraris and became internationally known as a racing driver, Parkes had achieved some fame in English motoring circles not only for his driving at club level but for his work on some remarkably advanced racing suspension design, and as an engineer on the rear-engined, independently suspended Hillman Imp saloon.

Colonel Hoare recommended Parkes for an engineer's post at Maranello and all parties benefited. The Colonel's Maranello Concessionaires agency now had an English friend at high level in the factory. Parkes found himself working on some of the world's most exciting road and racing cars (they must have made a change from the Rootes Group's Imp) and he had a works drive into the bargain, taking him eventually into a Formula 1 seat with Ferrari. Meanwhile Ferrari himself had at last found a designer who could make his road cars handle as well as they accelerated. It was a loss for many people when, some years after his sojourn at Ferrari and having moved to Lancia (by then both companies being Fiat subsidiaries), poor Michael Parkes was killed in a road accident.

The 275 benefited from his skill from end to end. At the front the traditional forged wishbones went, to be replaced by some less artistic pressed-steel wishbones that gave more modern suspension geometry. Coil springs were retained, enclosing Koni dampers.

At the rear beefy wishbones were again welded up from steel pressings, giving geometry close to that used for the racers. To maintain adequate ground clearance the lower wishbone was set quite high, with a massive upright connecting each to an upper wishbone that was almost at rim level. The coil spring/damper unit was placed above this upper wishbone, inclined inwards and mounted on the end of a multi-tubular frame carrying the rear suspension and of course the chassis-mounted gearbox/differential unit.

The casual observer would have concluded from a glance at this structure that the 275 had a proper racing-style space frame of the kind first seen on a road car back in the 1950s in the Mercedes-Benz 300SL Gullwing, but attempted by few manufacturers since due to its cost and complexity.

The impression would have been heightened had he looked under the bonnet of a 275 and spotted the truss members running along either side at the top of the engine bay.

He would, however, have been wrong. The 275's chassis is not much more advanced technically than that of the preceding 250s. It is basically a ladder frame that is actually more in the shape of a fly-swatter, broadening out beneath the cockpit where it has horizontal x-bracing, and narrowing between the rear wheels. It is built around two main oval-tube longerons, with

Above *Posed by Pininfarina
on a hilltop overlooking the
plains of Lombardy, the 1964
275GTB coupé was poised for
a near-four-year production
run during which it would
undergo two major
metamorphoses*

Left *The GTB in early guise,
with optional Borrani
wheels, a small rear window
and internal boot lid hinges.
The rear view was strongly
reminiscent of the GTO*

Above The interim model:
the coupé in second-series
form with the early (2-cam)
engine but the long-nosed
body later used for the
GTB/4

Right Uncomplicated,
flowing lines; voluptuous,
along bulbous curves,
reminiscent of 1960's styling,
were hallmarks of the
Pininfarina body design

991152-ROMA

Top *The GTS convertible got an altogether different, less exotic shape intended to harmonise with its role as a touring car rather than a café racer like the berlinetta* Above *Beneath the bonnet of the GTB/C lurked this odd carburetter arrangement. The cars had only three twin-choke Webers because the 6-carburetter option had yet to be homologated. Long ram pipes, to move the torque peak down the rev range, were curved to fit under the bonnet* Right *The extremely rare GTB/C, of which only a handful were built for competition use by private owners*

JAP 1D

Left *4-cam on the road. It drives, says the owner, like a racing car detuned for ordinary use—while other sports cars tend to feel like well developed versions of ordinary saloons*

Above Right *The archetypal Ferrari: a red 2-seat coupé with 12-cylinder engine. Collector Nick Mason bought this 275GTB/4 because it was the nearest thing among road cars to a full-blooded 250GTO*

Right *The ultimate Ferrari engine? The 3.3-litre, 4 ohc, 300 bhp, 8000 rpm V12 of a 275GTB/4*

In the mid-1960s competition 275s did well at Le Mans, humming smoothly round to finish well up in both the GT class and overall standings as out-and-out racers fell by the wayside. This works-prepared car did best of all, finishing third overall in 1965 in the hands of sometime Ferrari F1 driver Willy Mairesse and his fellow Belgian, Le Mans veteran 'Beurlys'.

Cooling was often a problem on these competition 275s and this car has received some summary surgery to admit more air

outriggers supporting the body and cockpit floor; the aforementioned sub-structure for the rear end; a hefty fabricated cross-member carrying the front suspension and steering, and some tubes welded into the engine compartment to stiffen things up a bit. The main requirement for location of these 'space frame' tubes seems to be one of wherever they will fit around the other components, rather than where they are needed. There is also a tubular sub-structure for the scuttle bulkhead.

Chassis design was not a Ferrari strong point in the 275 era. The front end superstructure, admittedly partly cut away in this workshop shot, was intended more to support the body and radiator than to add much strength to the basic frame

Above and Right *Early Ferraris had live rear axles. The 275 marked a major step forward, borrowing from competition technology and using sophisticated double wishbone layout. The wishbones themselves were built up from steel pressings. Clamped midway along the wishbone is the vertical link to the anti-roll bar. Brakes were no more prepossessing than those at the front*

On paper, then, the 275 chassis looks the kind of thing British designers were turning their backs on 10 years earlier, especially when seen against Jaguar's racing-derived monocoque/space frame for the E type.

The Ferrari chassis is simple and fairly cheap to make, even though the main tubes are relatively exotic: they are produced from an unusually fine grade of steel—and in an odd ovality of cross-section—that makes it hard for anyone other than the factory or its appointed agent to carry out proper repairs to crash damage. But stiff

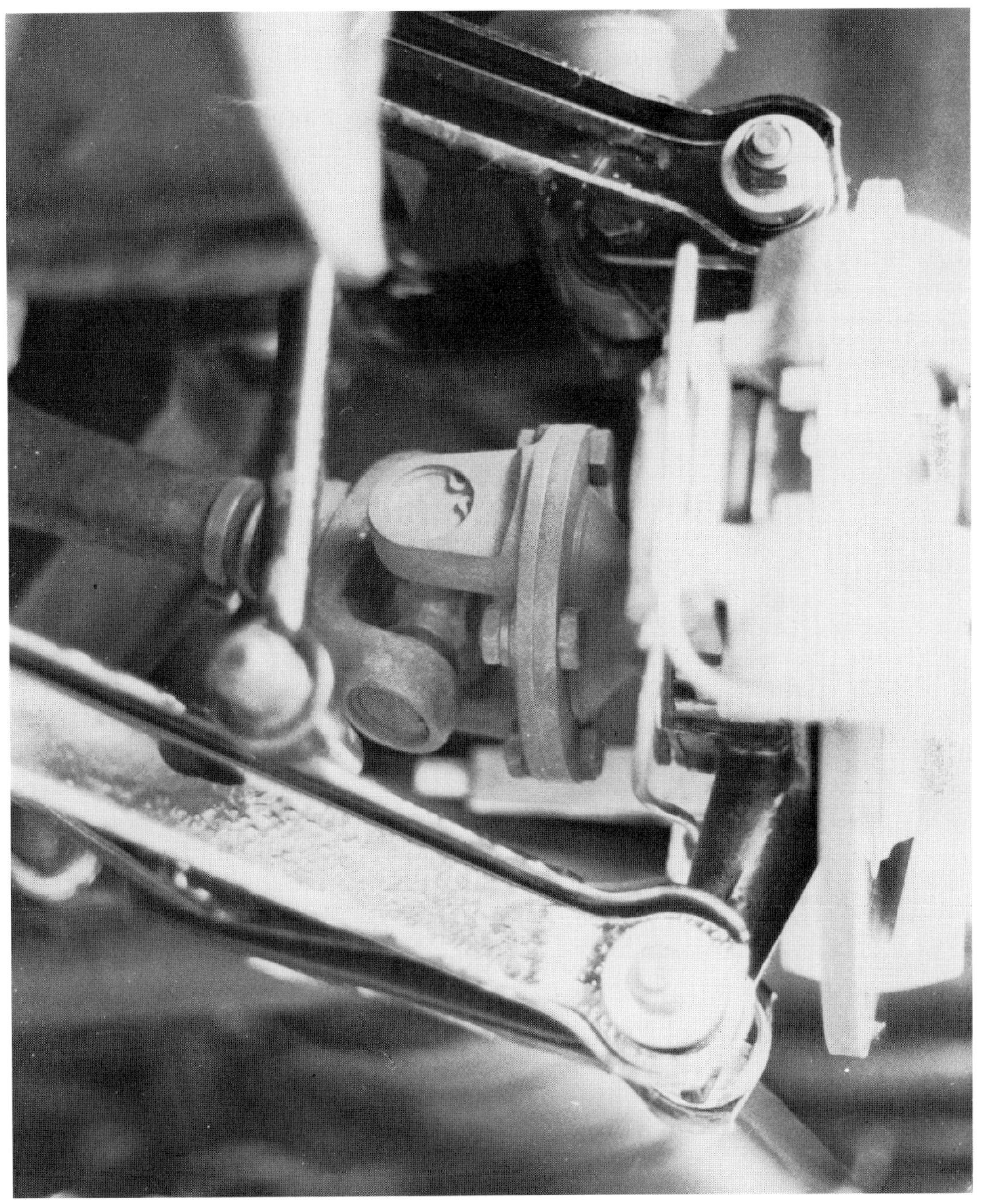

the chassis is not. Or so it would appear. In practice, however, the steel body adds considerably to the overall effect, making a body/chassis unit that is torsionally quite rigid. The rare GTBs with alloy bodywork, and the open 275GTS, are noticeably less taut when driven at all hard.

But academically correct or not, and Michael Parkes arrived at Ferrari too late to have much say in basic chassis design, they still—and this is the surprising thing—are possessed of far and away the best handling and roadholding of any cars of their kind.

Leaving aside the mid-engined machinery that came later, and forgetting racing GT cars like the GTO, the 275GTB is by common consent of drivers one of the best of its kind. And that is thanks to the development work put in by Parkes. He knew from his racing experience that if a basic design is acceptable, and the 275's was certainly that, careful development of suspension geometry (by altering wishbone lengths and pick-up points), spring rates, damper bounce and rebound resistance, and anti-roll bar stiffness (the 275 had anti-roll bars front and rear) can turn the merely acceptable into the excellent.

Most supposedly maintenance-free suspension bushes use rigid low-friction bearings to stop the wishbone pivoting longitudinally under braking; and at the rear, pivoting from high engine torque loads. The later cars had marginally more rubber in the bushes—and thus more compliance—but still felt remarkably taut, almost like a racing car, as a result of this no-compromise approach to suspension design. Wheelbase was a compact 7 ft 10.5 in, with front track of 4 ft 7 in and rear track of 4 ft 7.7 in.

The measure of Parkes's success can be felt as soon as you drive a 275. Despite weighing rather

over a ton it has the light steering, and instantaneous steering response, of a well-sorted 2-litre car. The basic handling characteristic itself is neutral—and that's quite an achievement in any front-engined car. The 275 goes where you point it, holding the chosen line perfectly on neutral throttle. Give it less power, so that it is on

The classic Borrani wheel: alloy rim, Rudge-Whitworth type hub and triple-eared spinner with a prancing horse embossed in the centre. Seen here on a GTB

Above and Right *Do Ferrari's rust? Wheel arches are a major rust spot, as are sills. These pictures of a 275 getting some comestic surgery also show the rear double wishbone set-up, with coil spring/damper unit mounted above the upper wishbone*

the overrun, and it oversteers gently. Give it more power and the turning circle tightens.

Ultimately, and under extreme provocation, one or other end will break free, of course. Whether it's the front or rear will depend entirely on how the driver has mismanaged the corner. But you have to be going very fast indeed for that to happen. When it does occur, though, it happens quickly and you have to be equally quick to retrieve the situation.

Rack-and-pinion steering came late to Italy, and although Parkes undoubtedly wanted to see something better, the 275 retains the outdated ZF

worm and peg layout of the 250 and its predecessors. However, he was able to improve it to a point at which accuracy and absence of lost motion is about on a par with rack-and-pinion systems, while absence of kickback from potholes and bumps is, if anything, better. The turning circle was an unwieldy 44 feet.

The damping is firm, to the point of making bumpy country lanes tiresome to drive on as the car fidgets over the bumps. And at low speeds the sensitive steering is all too ready to obey minor deflections imposed by those bumps. At higher speeds it absorbs the imperfections better, though. And on the open main road, where a Ferrari ought to be, it is pure joy to drive.

Pure joy, that is, until you need the brakes in a hurry. For some reason known only to Ferrari the 275 appeared with 14-in diameter wheels, and retained them throughout its life*. Most cars of its size and weight had 15s, and the 15-in was capable of accommodating a man-sized brake disc. The 14 was not, so the 275 was cursed with small, thin, solid discs (the ventilated kind being unknown on road cars then) that a designer of today might just consider suitable for, say, a 1600 cc saloon. They are of Dunlop manufacture and with them came a cast-iron Dunlop caliper that was so deep that it imposed further limitations on disc diameter, and yet so flexible that it spreads apart fractionally under heavy pressure loads, thus ensuring that all 275s have a permanently slightly spongy pedal.

Past or present owners of early Jaguar E types will know the problems, since their cars had a similar Dunlop system. Not long after the 275, Dunlop got out of the brake business altogether. ... Just to make matters worse, Ferrari incorporated into the system a locally made Bonaldi servo that was not exactly noted for its efficiency. The upshot of all this was that the 150 mph-plus 275 appeared with a definitely second-rate set of brakes. Fitted with standard pads they would work well enough under normal conditions, but could fade if used hard, while the pedal action and servo, as we have seen, were not of the best.

The handbrake is largely ineffective, as are most all-disc systems of the era, and is made more so by the fact that the lever is uncomfortably far away from the driver.

*Some competition versions used 15-in.

The problems were magnified when it came to the six-carburettor 275s and the 4-cam. Their greater speed capability put that much more strain on the already overworked discs. And in the 4-cam (and to a lesser extent the six-carb 2-cam) there was another, more serious problem: the vacuum servo is activated by a bleed from only one of the inlet stubs. The 275 does not use balance pipes to interconnect the carburettor/inlet tract assemblies, so on a six-carburettor installation the amount of vacuum available in one pair of stubs to operate the servo is at best minimal. On the 4-cam it becomes even less, because the race-profile cam allows such overlap that at low engine speeds there is frequently almost no vacuum available in the inlet anyway. So the already overworked, under-exhausted Bonaldi servo is occasionally brought to a state in which its reserves have been used up; yet there is insufficient engine vacuum available at that moment to recharge it. What memorable occasions these are.

Classically they occur on one of the hairier 275s when you slow from high speed (thus using up the reserve in the servo), then pull up to a stop line or traffic lights. For the second bit of braking there's just nothing left and suddenly the pedal goes hard and dead. Unless you have quick reflexes and leg muscles like a weight lifter's, the Ferrari sails majestically on. By the grace of God it hits nothing, but more than a few 275s are on their second or even third noses as a result of trundling unstoppably out into the traffic.

On a circuit—and most 275s find their way onto one sooner or later—the brake shortcomings show up even more. Vacuum shortage is no problem there, because the engine is turning fast enough to keep it up, but fade soon sets in. Take heart, though, from the fact that the 275 is not

Ferraris do rust! Doors are particularly corrosion prone, as this shot of the remains of a 275 door interior shows

alone: all Ferraris have inadequate brakes for their performance on a circuit: the Daytona, for instance, boils its fluid merrily, and even the modern Boxer soon runs into fade. On the road, though, it's just not possible (well, *seldom* possible) to drive a Ferrari fast enough for long enough to encounter these snags.

But back to the 275 and its own shortcomings. There is a cure and a highly effective one at that, evolved by Jock Bruce of Modena Engineering, Ferrari specialists in England's Surrey countryside. The Bonaldi servo is removed and cast into the night, to be replaced by a proper unit from Girling. Then a reservoir tank is tucked away in one of the front wings, ensuring that sufficient vacuum is always on hand. Finally, a mechanically driven servo pump (a Ferrari part, borrowed from another model) is fitted out of sight on the engine.

With these mods the 275 winds up with a perfectly acceptable braking system. The fade can be cured by switching to harder pads, although that's needed only on the track, where it throws up another problem—that of excessive heat in the discs themselves. And for the road at least one 275 4-cam has gone the other way and been fitted with softer Mintex M33 pads to improve low-speed response and overall pedal feel. These pads, it must be said, are that much more fade-prone on a circuit. Two brisk laps of Goodwood are enough to make them all but vanish.

What a pity, though, that Ferrari didn't stick to 15-in wheels and install the excellent brake system of the GTO. As it is, to alter wheel sizes now is too major a modification for most owners to consider. Not that a change of wheels would come amiss, perhaps, for the standard ones are magnesium castings of boring appearance. The first 275s had a not unpleasing ribbed-spoke effect and narrow 6.5-in rims. Later cars went to 7-in rims and changed to an ultra-simple wheel design derived from competition. These present a smoother outer surface with only a ring of rectangular holes to break the monotony. The poor old brake discs, tucked well away inside these deeply offset rims, could never have had a chance of keeping cool.

An alternative at extra cost was to order the car with Borrani wire wheels. Made by a small, independent company in Milan, these classics of the Italian sports car scene combine a polished alloy rim with an old-fashioned knock-on triple-eared spinner on a splined hub, connecting the two with a complex pattern of 72 double-butted spokes. They were standard on the GTS, an option on the GTB.

Exciting as they look, a wire wheel is stretched near the limits of its ability when supporting a one and a quarter ton car capable of the g forces a Ferrari can manage. Especially when shod with Michelins (Dunlop and Pirelli have also made tyres to suit 275s, but understandably lost interest in recent years), the 275 can load-up a wheel very heavily indeed. Couple to this the kind of torque that the 3.3-litre engine produces and it's not hard to see why the Borrani actually feels less rigid, than its cast counterpart, to the driver: a few thousand miles of enthusiastic use and the wheels need tightening and truing again.

Tyre wear can also be fairly heavy, even when using the excellent XWX Michelins that suit the 275 best. The sort of geometry that keeps the outside tyres so nicely vertical during enthusiastic cornering brings in its train a lot of tread-reducing scrub movement. Owners have to hope that Michelin will retain this tyre in production, which comes with the increasingly academic VR130-plus mph speed rating, the 205 × 14 size and an unfashionably high 82 per cent aspect ratio.

Chapter 6
Pininfarina and Scaglietti bodywork

While many other body designers have had a go from time to time, most notably Bertone, the story of Ferrari has really been that of master-stylist Pininfarina too. With only a very few exceptions all the truly classic Ferraris have been styled by him as the acknowledged maestro.

When it came to the 275 Pininfarina was at his best. The styling guidelines called for a car that could take over from two production 250GTs, the competition-orientated short-wheelbase berlinetta and the touring Lusso, yet had strong visual connections with the 250GTO racing models, both in their original 1962-63 form and in the later '64' model. At the same time, the new car had to continue the bloodline of two-seat Ferrari coupés that started with the Tour de France 250 of the mid-1950s.

So, with at least half the shape already delineated for him, Pininfarina had the task of coming up with something that combined the best of each earlier car in a single, elegant whole. He succeeded in marrying the rakish, long-bonneted look of the early GTOs with the vast, shallow-angled windscreen of the GTO/64. He then built in the sharply cut-off transom-style Kamm tail of these cars, spoiler lip and all, and yet related it to lightly razor-edged front wings that were harking back to the competition coupés of the 1950s. He completed the effect with a hint of the flowing, if slightly bulbous, curves of the Lusso.

The overall effect was one of traditional lines updated, rather than the new, not to say *nouveau riche* look, that Lamborghini was adopting at the time.

This basic shape was maintained throughout the 275's four-year production run, changing only in 1966 when the introduction of the torque-tube mechanical layout coincided with a lengthening of the nose and a slimming down of the air intake to improve aerodynamic stability at high speeds. The short-nose cars had shown a tendency to get disconcertingly light and wandery on the steering at over 130 mph.

At the same time the rear window was enlarged and the boot lid hinges, hitherto tucked away out of sight but a threat to suitcase tops, were mounted externally. As with some other minor Ferrari hardware of the time, these hinges came from the Alfa Romeo parts bin.

The only other change was the introduction of a raised centre to the bonnet when the 4-cam engine came along in 1967, to increase the air-cleaner clearance.

That then was the classic 275GTB shape. There were two other styles. First, you could have your 275 as a convertible, in which case Ferrari showed his usual relative lack of interest in open cars for the road by adopting a pleasant but uninspired Pininfarina convertible design, also used for the 330GTS drophead when this model replaced the 275GTS.

Much more glamorous was the open version of the GTB coupé, dreamed up by North American Ferrari importer Luigi Chinetti. This simply consisted of chopping the roof off the GTB and fitting a small hood. The overall look was almost identical to a one-off that the independent Neri e Bonacini body shop in Modena had earlier, in 1966, produced for a customer on a 250GT chassis. It was startlingly attractive.

Early rival from down the road: the original Lamborghini, also a V12 but pre-dating Ferrari in having four overhead camshafts for a road engine. The peculiar styling did nothing to help sales, however . . .

These late, 1964-type GTOs shared some styling features with the 275, notably the well-raked windscreen, narrowed roof and humped rear wings. These two are at Reims in 1964. Note their individual styling

These 'open GTBs', generally called 275GTS/4 NART* Spiders after Chinetti's North American Racing Team, were built in limited numbers, but as is so often the case a few years after the event, no one today is quite clear just how many, various sources quoting anything between nine and 25. In view of their extreme rarity (there are apparently only two in Europe—one in Spain, the other in England) it seems likely that Chinetti planned on 25, but only managed to sell the nine.

*The factory also referred to them as the 275GTB/4 NART.

Long-nose, 2-cam 275 in street form. Most owners omitted wing mirrors for fear of spoiling the svelte lines. This one didn't

Late 2-cam GTBs and all 4-cammers had this rear end treatment with large window, external boot hinges and the customary Kamm-type cut off tail featuring a GTO-style spoiler

A competition GTB, fitted with Borrani's outward-laced wheels at the front and extra wide rims at the rear

The cockpit of a long-nose 275 (sometimes referred to by Ferraristi as the GTB/2). Many owners have disconnected and removed the choke. A few stabs of the throttle richen the mixture enough for a cold start even in winter

Although designed by Pininfarina, the 275 bodies were actually built in Modena at the factory of Scaglietti. Today yet another subsidiary of Fiat, the Scaglietti business was in those days owned as well as run by the Ferrari factory. It was responsible for more of Ferrari production than was generally realised, since the chassis frames were built there alongside the

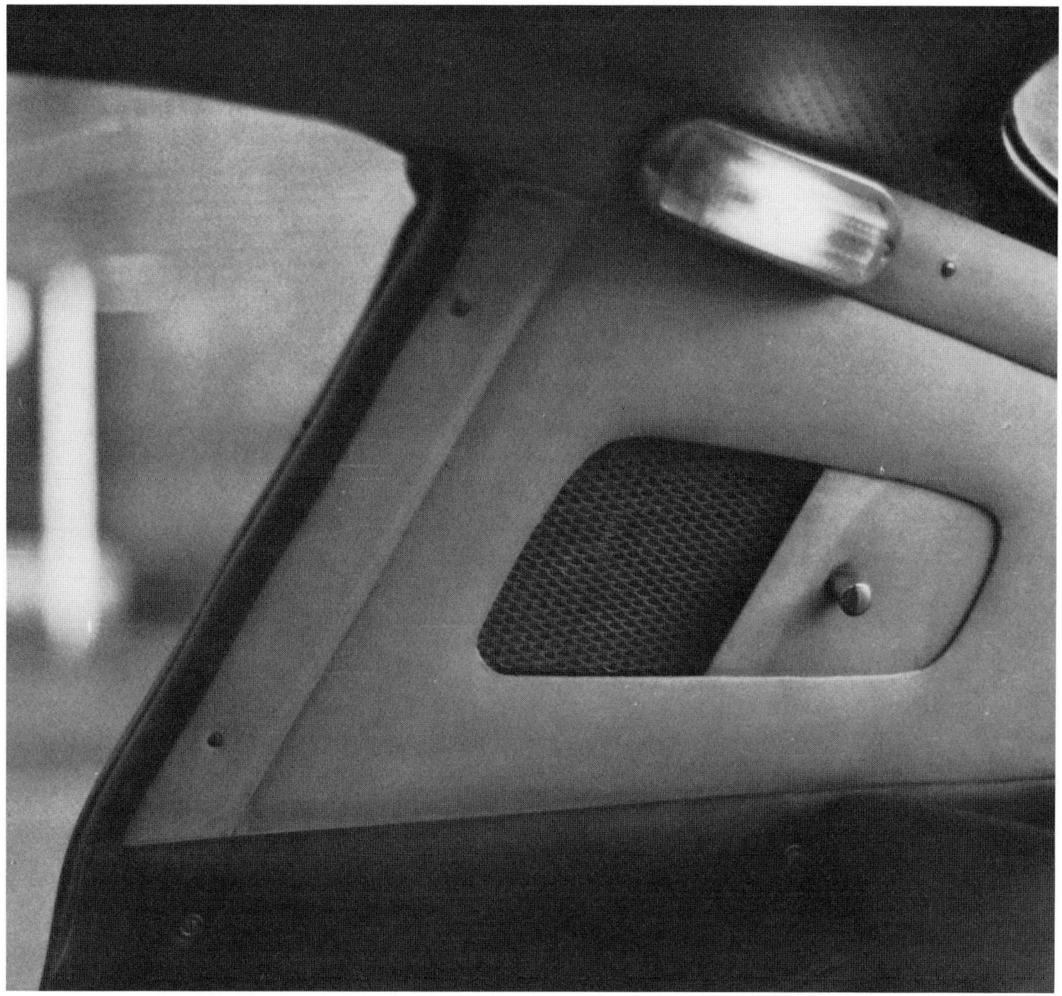

Part of a rudimentary ventilation system, sliding covers that give onto vents in the roof quarter panels

bodies, and the two units were married up before being loaded onto lorries for the trip out into the country to the Ferrari plant at Maranello. There the car's Ferrari-made mechanical components were installed before it was trucked back to Scaglietti for finishing.

Potentially a styling house itself, had it been given the chance, Scaglietti had designed the

The classic 275, the GTB/4 revealing a profile descended from the 250GT Europa/ Berlinetta/Lusso/GTO bloodline to this rakish final form

The S in production form. The convertible version of the 275 bore no visual relation whatsoever to its coupé brother, having sober lines—and a less highly tuned engine that underlined Ferrari's view of the convertible as more of a boulevard car and less of a near-racer

classic pontoon-fendered Ferrari Testa Rossa sports-racer and had had a hand too in the basically factory-styled GTO. However, for the GTBs the company was allowed only to follow Pininfarina's bidding. All panels were hand made, Ferrari production runs being far too short to justify the vast cost of presses; and the most complicated tools were usually a set of panel-beaters' hammers and blocks of wood on which to form the panels. All 275s were normally bodied in steel, with alloy doors, bonnet and boot lid. Full alloy bodywork was available at extra cost.

As a result no two Ferraris, 275s included, are quite alike. For example one may have more pronounced razor edges to the wings, another a deeper roof. In fact they are not even symmetrical in many cases: close inspection reveals perhaps slightly more fullness in one wing, or a thinning out on one side of a panel that is more rounded on the opposite side.

All this, it must be said, is no criticism—merely observation of an endearing characteristic.

What does bear criticism, though, is the

dreadful proneness to rust of these and most other Ferraris. Partly as a result, it is thought, of using rather low-grade steel for the bodies, and partly because water-traps abound, corrosion is a continuing problem for the owner. Typically, after a few years a 275 will need new sills, fresh metal in the wheel arches and around the wing tops, and may be suffering too from electrolytically induced corrosion where alloy door and bonnet skins are wrapped around steel tube frames. The only answer will be familiar to any boat owner: constant maintenance and the occasional expensive overhaul of the 'hull'.

One other snag persists with the coupés, though not on the open-headlight convertibles: moulded plastic fairings enclose the headlights. They mist up in damp weather and the plastic itself, being at approximately 45 degrees to the light source, greatly reduces the power and accuracy of the headlamp beam.

Although an expensive car when new the GTB was surprisingly skimpily trimmed and equipped in the cockpit. This was in keeping with Ferrari tradition, the luxury touches being kept for the 4-

An early version of Pininfarina's GTS, lacking the vents in the front wings that later became standard

275 line-up outside the premises of Modena Engineering in Surrey, England. From left to right: short nose GTB, GTS and GTB/4

Above *The GTS's hood folds away in true convertible style to tuck down behind the rear seats. This model was aimed at a customer not expected to accept a clip-on hood with separate sticks*

Right *Cockpit of a GTS, showing the classic dash layout, gated gearlever, inaccessible handbrake (most drivers can't reach while wearing a seat belt) and passenger footrest*

Above *The GTS rear end, with typically vestigial quarter-bumpers and the exhaust suspended (as it is throughout its length) on rubber straps*

Left *While the coupés had GTO-like vertical air vents in the front wings, only just above sill level, the GTS convertible had these higher mounted slots*

103

The definitive shape of the series 2 GTB, the long-nose, torque-tube model. Main visual changes were to extend the nose and reduce the air intake, improving aerodynamic stability; to fit the uninspiring slotted wheels and to enlarge the rear window, while adding external boot hinges

PININFARINA AND SCAGLIETTI—BODYWORK

litre cars. Thus although the seats and some trim panels were in leather, much of the cockpit lining was in perforated leathercloth. Early cars had vinyl seats with cloth inserts, full leather becoming available later.

One New York customer, Dan del Rio, ordered his GTB/4 (The *Automobile Quarterly* test car) with Connolly hide throughout, for this was in the days when the factory was still happy to indulge a customer's whims. Mr del Rio also specified an enormous externally mounted racing filler cap, and ram pipes instead of the usual vast air-

A 275GTB/C in 1965. Note the wraparound rear window, flattened roofline and no chrome trim on the windscreen and rear window—rather nice. Not to much is known about this 'special'. It was a factory car with its Prova plates

Back in Italy in 1967. The 275GTS/4 NART with hood up on the left contrasts with the brand new, first off, 365 California cabriolet on the right. Both for the American enthusiast . . .

The 275 GTS/4 NART, conceived by US importer Luigi Chinetti for a West Coast market that enjoyed suitable weather for spiders. The car was a simple convertible development, by Scaglietti, of the standard 4-cam coupé.

cleaner for the carburettors. Also to heighten the competition look further, he had the bumpers removed and their mounting holes filled in. The latter were probably no great loss: with consideration more for how they looked than how they worked, the thinly chromed bumpers were bolted direct onto the body panels they supposedly protect.

On some cars the passenger was given a

substantial hinged foot rest in the form of a bar across the end of the footwell.

Behind the seats is a carpeted platform, big enough for overnight bags but no more, and with two heavy straps to retain luggage. The boot itself could just manage a couple of small suitcases plus some odds and ends.

Heating and ventilation are rudimentary. Vague controls set the air temperature and direct

Another shot of those taken during the NART Spider's press launch. Everything's perfect . . . in the background there is an unconcerned citizen reading his paper on a park bench during this historic occasion

Above *Plenty of work even for a skilled craftsman. This 275 rolled off the freeway in California. Whether it was restored to its original condition (better, in fact) or converted into a Spider is not known*

Right *It must have seemed a good idea at the time. At least one American bodyshop will convert your GTB into a pseudo NART Spider, as is being done here. Are the roofs saved just in case the customer changes his mind?*

its flow to windscreen or foot level, aided by separately switched fans for left and right. Two vents with sliding covers in the scuttle flanks can be opened to bring in cold air, and two in the rear quarter panels supposedly let it out again. In the summer the same kind of heat that makes fuel vaporise under the bonnet also overheats the driver and passenger. Cockpit cooling, other than by opening the windows (a very few cars had electric windows) or quarterlights, is totally inadequate.

The driving position is superb, at least if you are shaped in the supposed Italian mould with relatively short legs and long trunk and arms. Since the seat back cannot be reclined on the

GTB, it's fairly important to be that way, although one British 275 owner with longer legs overcame the problem by ordering his car from the factory with reclining-back seats from a luxury Ferrari installed.

The steering wheel is the classic wood-rimmed, alloy 3-spoked kind, with a black prancing horse on the yellow horn button. The longish gear lever in its visible gate looks to be too far away, but in practice is just where you want it. Visibility is good ahead and astern, but poor to the sides due to the lack of rear quarter glass.

The dash is trimmed in leather on the later cars, replacing a teak surround for the instruments on early versions. A traditional instrument layout is used, with the big Veglia rev counter and speedometer that Italian car makers love, the oil

114

pressure and oil temperature gauges between them, right below the driver's normal sight line, and then instruments for water temperature, ammeter and fuel level, plus a clock, away over the centre of the dash. Beneath them are rocker switches for the fans, heated rear window, interior light, master lights control (dip and main beam being on one of the three steering column stalks—the others are wiper and washer action plus turn signals) and the electric fuel pump needed to prime the carburettors before starting from cold and to clear fuel vapour lock on hot days. Dashboards of this traditional design come in for equally traditional criticism from magazine road testers, but it must be said that an owner soon accustoms himself to any vagaries of design and can find the switch he seeks when he needs it.

Chapter 7
Would it race?

By the advent of the 275GTB the gap between road cars and GT racers had widened to a point at which it could never be bridged again. You could drive a GTO to and from a meeting quite happily. But the 250LM, also supposedly a GT car, was a very impractical proposition anywhere but on a circuit.

Nonetheless, several 275 customers wanted to go racing, more or less seriously, and for these people Maranello produced the 275GTB/C. This car had high-lift cams, larger valves (borrowed from the 250LM), bigger carburettors, stronger crankshaft and pistons, dry-sump lubrication, thin-gauge aluminium body, Plexiglas side and

Full-house 275 GTB/C at the Nürburgring in 1965. In this version the factory-prepared alloy-bodied racer featured a more penetrating nose, à la GTO, wide-rimmed wheel, extra louvres to remove brake cooling air in the enlarged rear wings, and a neat bonnet bulge for the carburettors on the full-race engine. Extra spotlights were faired in for night racing

rear windows, wider wheels and flared wheel arches. About 10, possibly 12, cars were built, mostly for private owners, although a few were retained by the factory. One of these, entered by Britain's Maranello Concessionaires, finished a fine eighth overall and first in the GT class at Le Mans in 1966, driven by Roy Pike and the late Piers Courage.

The GTB/C of Zwimpfer en route up the mountain in the 1967 Freiburg-Schauinsland climb. Like most other Cs, this one had competition Borranis with the outer ring of spokes laced into the edge of the rim

275 drivers even tried their
hand at rallying, as witness
the much modified B of
Pianta and Lippi in the 1966
Monte Carlo. Note the
battery of spotlights

Left *One of the most active private entrants of a 275, British enthusiast Paul Vestey at the 1967 Spa 1000 km. Vestey took in a number of long-distance sports car events, including Le Mans*

A number of other 275s were put into competition specification by the factory, although with fewer changes than those made to achieve the GTB/C.

Maranello also went further with some of the 275s for its own use. These featured revised bodywork, with a more GTO-like nose, and the rear wings upswept into a higher tail than on the road cars. Following normal Ferrari factory practice, these cars were lent to foreign concessionaires to race. One, on loan to Ecurie Francorchamps (run by Belgian importer Jacques Swaters), came through to finish third overall and first in the GT class at the 1965 Le Mans, driven by Belgians Willy Mairesse and Jean Blaton, who raced under the name 'Beurlys'. Another driven by Charlie Kolb, won the Nassau Tourist Trophy that year. And one GTB, driven by Bandini, lapped the Nürburgring in practice in a remarkable 8:54.9 seconds, beating Surtees's race record of the previous year. In the race in the hands of both Baghetti and Biscaldi it was slower. In the factory yearbook Ferrari blandly described it as 'a normal berlinetta GTB. . . .'

The 275 never was, but then it never was intended to be, a successful racing car.

Far Left *275s were fairly popular with Italian privateers, including some of those who made up the numbers in the Targa Florio. Here the near-standard GTB of Conti-Venturi accelerates out of one of the Targa's innumerable mountain hairpins. The car recorded a DNF in this 1966 event*

CA

Chapter 8
The era ends

This book is one highly personalised view on a car which, even allowing for the occasional blemish, must rank as an all-time classic. At its ultimate, in GTB/4 form, I would say that the 275 has had no equal since as a driving machine for giving pleasure on open roads. It probably had only a single counterpart in terms of 'drivability' from the pre-war era, too, in the form of the straight-eight Type 59 Bugatti; a racing two-seater, coincidentally of 3.3 litres, which was very occasionally put on the road. Like the Type 59 before it, the 275 may not have had an outstanding competition record, but as a road machine it had no peer. With no slight intended, and borrowing a phrase from motorcyling parlance, it was the best café racer ever produced.

The 275 went out of production in early 1968, killed off because the all-important Amercian market was closed to cars that did not meet an increasingly unrealistic set of smog and safety regulations. It was the end of an era. The 275 was the architype Ferrari for the road, the last model to be produced before the Fiat influence began to be felt, the last direct product of a unique figure in motoring. There were still buyers around, even when the 4-cam cost in Britain a heady £6515 against the £1967 price tag on, say, a new E type. But Ferrari enthusiasts would have nearly two years to wait for another two-seater coupé from Maranello in the form of the Daytona. And that

The last of the first heads the first of, well, the next generation: a 275 4-cam with, behind, a Daytona

After the elegant 275s came the brute-strength Daytona, seen here holding up an angry Matra at Le Mans

was a car which, for all its speed, lacked the GTB's charisma.

Collector Nick Mason sums it up in his own reasons for buying a 4-cam: 'I went for the 275 because it was the nearest thing you could get to the 250GTO and I couldn't find a GTO at that time. [An omission Mr Mason has subsequently rectified.] It had near-GTO handling and performance, without the drawbacks on the road of a real competition car. And it looked beautiful. It was noisy, too much so to make a radio worth having, but it was the right kind of noise.

'The 4-cam was a confidence-inspiring car:

entering a difficult 120 mph bend at 121 mph you knew it would come out all right. And the brakes at those speeds were fine. But around town they were so bad as to be ludicrous, until we modified them to cure the servo problem.

'Compared to a Daytona, the 275 has nothing like the comfort and convenience—no air conditioning, no electric windows (at least on my car), and very little sound-insulation. And you miss the Daytona's vast torque. But for sheer driving enjoyment I still love this car.'

Ferrari connoisseur Mike Salmon endorses Nick's view. Having owned Ferraris, raced

Red-blooded racing relative of the front-engined 275 road cars, this mid-engined 250LM shared a little of the looks (in the vast windscreen) and design layout (both cars utilised double wishbone suspension all round)

them—at Le Mans and elsewhere in a long and successful motor sporting career—and sold them when a director of Maranello Concessionaires he is particularly well qualified to appreciate these cars. The model that he chose to keep, laying it down almost like a vintage wine, except that it sees regular use, is a silver-grey 275 4-cam. It has been restored to a condition that makes it the best in Europe, possibly in the world. He has turned down offers for this car of 50 per cent and more over the market price. So he should have the last word. 'It's quite simple: the *true* Ferrari is a front-engined, 12-cylinder, two-seat coupé.' None more so than the 275GTB.

Left That trite old cliche about racing improving the breed has some meaning at Maranello: this 275P2 at the Nürburgring 1000 km in 1965 has a power unit closely related to that of the road cars

Specifications

Years of production	GTB, 1964–67
	GTS, 1964–65
	GTB/C, 1965–66
	GTB/4, 1967–68
Numbers built*	GTB, 465
	GTS, 200
	GTB/4, 280

Engine
Type	2-cam, Type 213
	4-cam, Type 226
No. of cylinders	V12 in 60 degree vee
Bore & stroke	77 × 58.8 mm
Capacity	3285.7 cc
Cylinder heads	Light alloy
Valve gear	GTB, GTS, GTB/C: two sohc (2-cam)
	GTB/4: two dohc (4-cam)
Cylinder block	Light alloy
No. of main bearings	7
Lubrication	GTB & GTS, wet sump
	GTB/4 & GTB/C, dry sump
Engine oil capacity	Sump, 10 litres (2.6 Imp gal)
	Tank, 16 litres (4.2 Imp gal)
Compression ratio	GTB, 9.2:1
Power/engine speed	GTB, 3-carb: 280 bhp/7600 rpm
	GTB, 6-carb: 300 bhp/7500 rpm
	GTS, 3-carb: 260 bhp/7600 rpm
	GTB/4: 300 bhp/8000 rpm

*All figures approximate, made up of GTB: 250 short nose, 205 long nose; 10 GTB/C; 9 NART Spiders

Carburation	GTB, 3-carb: Weber 40 DCZ/6 GTB, 6-carb: Weber 40 DCN/3, then 9 GTS: Weber 40 DCL/6 GTB/C: Weber 40 DFI/3 GTB/4: Weber 40 DCN/17

Transmission

Clutch	Fitchel and Sachs single plate, then Borg & Beck diaphragm
Gearbox	Ferrari 5-speed, transaxle, plus reverse
Differential	Ferrari transaxle with limited slip diff., then ZF diff.

Specifications

Chassis	Oval tube platform
Body	Steel except GTB/C and some specials
Suspension front	Unequal-length pressed-steel wishbones, coil springs over Koni shock absorbers. Independent. Anti-roll bar
rear	Transaxle, universally jointed and splined half-shafts with unequal-length wishbones, coil springs over Koni shock absorbers. Independent. Anti-roll bar
Brakes	Servo-assisted dual circuit
front	Solid discs
rear	Solid discs
Wheels	Early cars; Campagnolo magnesium alloy 'starburst', 14×6.5 rim. Later cars; light alloy 'slotted', 14×7 rim. GTS and optional; Borrani wire spoke, 14×6.7 or 7 rim
Tyres	Pirelli or Dunlop 195×14; then 205×14 often Michelin

Dimensions

Wheelbase, 94.5 in
Height, GTB: 60 in
GTS: 50 in
Width, GTB: 68 in
GTS: 66 in
Weight, GTB: 2425 lb*
GTS: 2535 lb

*Steel body

Production

'Late' 1964

275GTB introduced as replacement for the 250GT series. Subsequently known as 'short nose'. Production continued until late 1965. Approximately 250 cars built. Convertible (GTS) version produced at the same time, also discontinued in 'late' 1965, approximately 200 built.

1965

Competition version, generally the 275GTB/C, although some other variants not so named also appeared, introduced. Continued to be available into 1966. Approximately 10 built.

Spring 1966

Second-series GTB launched. Main changes were elongated nose ('long nose') and adoption of torque tube to link rigidly the front-mounted engine and the rear-mounted gearbox/final drive unit. Six-carburettor option. Larger rear window, and boot lid hinges moved to external position to increase luggage room. Approximately 205 cars built.

Spring 1967

'Single cam' GTB replaced by 275GTB/4 (also known as 275GTB/4A). Main changes: new twin-cam-per-bank cylinder heads, dry sump lubrication. Approximately 280 cars built by the time production ended in 'early' 1968.

1967

Small run of convertible version of GTB/4, commissioned by US importer Luigi Chinetti and known as NART Spider. Approximately 9 cars built, primarily for American customers but possibly including a few sold in Europe.

Acknowledgements

Special thanks are due from the author to Jock Bruce, Nick Mason and Michael Salmon for their help in the compilation of this book; to fellow-enthusiast Mike Pearman for his encouragement; and to Leonard Setright for reviving my enthusiasm for the 275 on those occasions when it wanes.

The publisher needs to extend his gratitude to many who contributed illustrations. Firstly to Mirco Decet who took many of the photographs especially for this book and to those owners of 275s who kindly loaned their cars for photography. Then to all the others, in alphabetical order; Rob de la Rive Box, David Clarke of Graypaul Motors Ltd., Peter Coltrin, Ferrari SpA SEFAC, Brian Joscelyn, Mark Konig of Maranello Concessionaires Ltd., Rick McCormack of The Newport Press, LAT, Carrozzeria Pininfarina, *Road & Track*, Stanley Rosenthall, Mike Sheeham of European Auto Restoration, Jerry Sloniger, Jonathan Thompson, Franco Varisco, Ernest A. Weil and Kurt Wörner.

Index